Golden Age of Piracy
on
Cape Cod
and in
New England

THEODORE PARKER BURBANK

Dead men tell no tales by Howard Pyle

Pirates fight on the beach by N.C. Wyeth, 1926

Golden Age of Piracy

on

Cape Cod

and in

New England

Theodore Parker Burbank

Salty Pilgrim Press
www.SaltyPilgim.com

Pirates watch their mates fight to the death
By Howard Pyle 1899

ISBN 978-1-935616-09-2

Cover design by G Scott B
Sunshine Joy
Woonsocket, RI

For additional copies or more information, please contact:

Salty Pilgrim Press
17 Causeway Street
Millis, MA 02054 USA
1 508 794 - 1200
captain@saltypilgrim.com

First Edition

Printed in the USA

One more step and I'll blow your brains out
by N.C. Wyeth - 1911

Forward

Three separate time periods between the 1650s and the 1730s have been referred to as "The Golden Age of Piracy." The Golden Age on Cape Cod and in New England was between the years 1690 and 1730 and encompassed two of the piratical eras:

- The "Pirate Round" of the 1690s, describes the period of the long-distance voyages from the Americas (primarily Providence, RI) and Bermuda to rob Muslim and East India Company targets in the Indian Ocean and Red Sea,

- The post War of Spanish Succession period, between 1714 to 1726, when Anglo-American sailors and privateers left unemployed by the end of the War of the Spanish Succession turned en masse to piracy in the Caribbean, the American eastern seaboard, the West African coast, and the Indian Ocean. It was during this period that a Pirate Republic at New Providence and the Pirate's Flying "Gang" was established.

New Providence

The "Brotherhood" is a monocle that is used to describe a pirate or a band of pirates such as those active in our chosen time frame. Our pirates went so far as to establish their own republic at New Providence in the Bahamas. They controlled and governed the island until the British sent an armed force to regain control. In the meantime New Providence provided our pirates safe haven from which to pillage and rob shipping and commerce around the world

The Flying Gang

Our pirates all new each other and belonged to what they called the Flying Gang. They had served to together; some as privateers, others in a Navy or as a seaman. The Flying Gang knew no boundaries. No sea was safe. They reign with fear, bound only to the wind, the brotherhood, and their ships. Some of the most famous pirates of the era were Edward "Blackbeard" Theach, Bartholomew "Black Bart" Roberts, Samuel "Black Sam" Bellamy.

Burning ship
By Howard Pyle Originally published in Collier's Weekly, circa 1898

Table of Contents

What you should know about pirates 1

Sample Pirate's Articles of Agreement 4

Punishment 5

History of Piracy 6

Pirate's Disability Pay 7

Pirate Myths 9

Ships of the Era 11

Pirate Weapons 14

Other Names for Pirates 15

The Brass Monkey and Cold Weather Debate 16

Pirate Flags 17

Golden Age of Piracy Begins in Rhode Island 19

Rhode Island, a Pirate's Haven 20

Pirates, Privateers, and Smuggling 21

Richest Piracy in History Plotted at Newport's
White Horse Tavern 24

The Pirate Fleet Assembles 26

The Biggest Prize in History 27

Thomas Tew – Native RI Pirate 28

Henry Every – Captures Millions - Disappears 30

Britain Moves Against Pirates 32

Pirates Executed 33

Pirates Last Roll Call 34

The Golden Age of Piracy & New Providence 35

Benefits of Becoming a Pirate 41

Pirates Create Their Own Republic 42

The Golden Age begins to Tarnish 44

King Sends Woodes Roger 46

Clemency for Pirates Proclaimed 48

The "Flying Gang" Pirates 53

How the "Flying Gang" Began 54

Flying Gang Connections 60

The Cape Cod and New England Connection 61

Forbes List of the Top Earning Pirates 62

The Most Famous Pirate? 65

Captain Kidd's Buried Treasure 71

Pirate Hornigold's Pirate Vocational Trainees 73

Benjamin Hornigold 74

The Flying Gang established 78

"Black Sam" Bellamy 87

The Saga of "Goody" Hallett 89

The beginning of Bellamy's pirating career 93

Was "Black Sam" Tricked into Eternity? 97

I'm From the Government and I'm Here to Help 99

Legend of "Goody's" Buried Treasure 100

The *Only* Pirate Treasure Ship Ever Recovered 101

Palgrave Williams – RI's "Royal" Pirate 110

Blackbeard the Pirate 115

Captain Howell Davis 122

Oliver Levasseur (La Buse) 123

Thomas Cocklyn 129

Bartholomew "Black Bart" Roberts 131

Protégés of Blackbeard 143

Stede Bonnet 144

Black Caesar 147

Protégés of Black Bart 149

Thomas Arstis 150

Walter Kennedy 153

Christopher Moody 155

Protégés of Thomas Arstis 157

John Phillips 158

Protégés of John Phillips 165

John Rose Archer 166

Protégés of Henry Jennings 167

Charles Vane 168

Protégés of Charles Vane 175

"Calico Jack" Rackman 176

Protégés of "Calico Jack" Rackham 179

Mary Read 180

Anne Bonny 183

Protégés of "Black Sam" Bellamy 187

Henry Jennings 188

Non "Flying Gang" Pirates in NE Waters   191

Joe Bradish   192

Jack Quelch   193

Thomas Pound   194

Ned (Edward) Low   197

Charles Harris   199

Philip Ashton   201

William Fly   202

Legend of Nix's Mate Island   204

The Curse of Nix's Mate   205

George and Rachael Wall   206

Charles Gibbs   208

Edward (Seegar) England   212

Where Treasure has Been Found in NE   213

Locations Where Pirates Have Buried Treasure on Cape Cod   214

Hannah Screecham – the Witch of Grand Island   215

Legends of Treasure – Where it Might be Found   219

Cape Cod Legends   220

Treasure on the Isles of Shoals   227

Pirate Sandy Gordon's White Isle Treasure   231

The Blood Red Rubies of Boon Island   237

Treasure in Casco Bay   239

Treasure in Penobscot Bay   249

Treasure in Boothbay   253

Treasure in Mid Coast Maine   255

Treasure in Macias Region   257

Finding relics and Old Coins   259

Pirates Use "Magic Rods" to Locate Treasure   261

Finding Treasure on Beaches   264

Resources   265

Other Books by Ted Burbank   267

Captain William Kidd Buries Treasure
By Howard Pyle - 1898

What You Should Know About Pirates

Pirate Ships were a Democracy

Democratic societies were the exception during the 'Golden Age of Piracy'. Europe was ruled by aristocratic kings and queens whose whims were the law. Similarly, the commands of a captain at sea were undisputable, and any infraction or deviation was met with harsh penalties.

Sea captains were known to be extremely brutal and often fed their crews rotten and maggot infested foods. Sailors frequently suffered from scurvy and other nutrition depravation-based disorders. Many crew members were aboard because they had been forcibly conscripted into service. The horrid living conditions and brutality of the captain and his officers caused many sailors of the day to develop a severe intolerance for absolute authority.

Pirates Elected Their Officers and Captain

A pirate ship functioned as a democracy with each crewman having an equal vote concerning operation of the ship. The crew had the power and the right to replace their leaders for any reason.

A major exception to this rule by mutual agreement was during battle when the captain's word was the undisputable law and any deviation from his command could result in death. The following is an excerpt from a pirate's trial in 1721 in London's Old Bailey.

Pirates voting

"They choose a captain from amongst themselves, who in effect held little more than that title, excepting in an engagement, when he commanded absolutely and without control. At all other times, the captain heeded the wishes of his crew."

Some suggest that portions of the pirate ship's model of a democratic society can be found in America's constitution. The most exact example could be the U.S. President becoming Commander in Chief of all the armed forces in times of war.

The ship's quartermaster was the officer with the real power over the commerce of the ship when not in battle. It was the quartermaster who kept the records of the booty and who was in charge of assuring its fair distribution amongst the crew. He, therefore, had to be trusted and respected by the crew. He also had to be somewhat educated as the position required that he posses the ability to read, write and compute.

Articles of Agreement or Pirate's Code

Life aboard a pirate ship was governed by rules originally called the Chasse-Partie or Charter Party and later referred to as Articles of Agreement, or Code of Conduct. All hands were required to sign on before they could join the crew.

Articles of Agreement

To become a full-fledged member of the crew each person was required to sign or make his mark plus swear an oath of allegiance. The swearing ceremony usually involved a Bible; however, crossed pistols, swords or a human skull were known to be used as well.

When a ship was captured, its crew members could elect to sign on as full-fledged members of the crew and share equally in the booty. Some would refuse and be pressed or be forced to be pirates anyway. However, if captured they would not be found guilty of piracy because they had not signed the articles.

3

Sample Pirate's Articles of Agreement

The Captain is to have two full Shares; the Master is to have one Share and a half; the Doctor, Mate, Gunner & Boatswain, one Share and a quarter.

I. Every man shall have an equal vote in affairs of moment. He shall have an equal title to the fresh provisions or strong liquors at any time seized, and shall use them at pleasure unless a scarcity may make it necessary for the common good that a retrenchment may be voted.

II. Every man shall be called fairly in turn by the list on board of prizes, because over and above their proper share, they are allowed a shift of clothes. But if they defraud the company to the value of even one dollar in plate, jewels or money, they shall be marooned. If any man rob another he shall have his nose and ears slit, and be put ashore where he shall be sure to encounter hardships.

III. None shall game for money either with dice or cards.

IV. The lights and candles should be put out at eight at night, and if any of the crew desire to drink after that hour they shall sit upon the open deck without lights.

V. Each man shall keep his piece, cutlass and pistols at all times clean and ready for action.

VI. No boy or woman to be allowed amongst them. If any man shall be found seducing any of the latter sex and carrying her to sea in disguise he shall suffer death.

VII. He that shall desert the ship or his quarters in time of battle shall be punished by death or marooning.

VIII. None shall strike another on board the ship, but every man's quarrel shall be ended on shore by sword or pistol in this manner. At the word of command from the quartermaster, each man being previously placed back to back, shall turn and fire immediately. If any man do not, the quartermaster shall knock the piece out of his hand. If both miss their aim they shall take to their cutlasses, and he that draweth first blood shall be declared the victor.

IX. No man shall talk of breaking up their way of living till each has a share. Every man who shall become a cripple or lose a limb in the service shall have 800 pieces of eight from the common stock and for lesser hurts proportionately.

IX   The captain and the quartermaster shall each receive two shares of a prize, the master gunner and boatswain, one and one half shares, all other officers one and one quarter, and private gentlemen of fortune one share each.

X   The musicians shall have rest on the Sabbath Day only by right. On all other days by favour only.

These were the Articles of Captain George Lowther, & his company

Punishment

Below is a list of the punishments metered out to pirates at their trial at Nijenburg in 1763 revealing the severity of the penalties at the time.

Sentenced to breaking on the wheel; hanged.
Sentenced to breaking on the wheel; broken on the wheel.
Sentenced to 3 times keelhauling, 200 lashes, and public humiliation; 3 times keelhauled, 200 lashes, banished.
Sentenced to death; 3 times keelhauled, 200 lashes, publicly humiliated.
Sentenced to death; thrown 3 times from the main mast, 150 lashes, banished.
Hanged, then beheaded.
Sentenced to hanging; lashed, burn-marked, lost his wage, banished.
Sentenced to breaking on the wheel and strangulation. His corpse was not allowed a burial.
Sentenced to hanging; was lashed, branded, and received 25 years of forced labour.
Beheaded.
Hanged, then beheaded.

Notice that rehabilitation is not on the list.

History of Piracy

The history of piracy dates back more than 3,000 years, but its accurate account depends on the actual meaning of the word 'pirate'. In English, the word piracy has many different meanings and its usage is still relatively new. Today, some uses of the word have no particular meaning at all. A meaning was first ascribed to the word piracy sometime before the XVII century. It appears that the word pirate (peirato) was first used in about 140 BC by the Roman historian Polybius.

The Greek historian Plutarch, writing in about 100 A.D., gave the oldest clear definition of piracy. He described pirates as those who attack without legal authority not only ships but also maritime cities. Piracy was described for the first time, in Homer's "The Iliad" and "The Odyssey". For a great many years there remained no unambiguous definition of piracy. Norse riders of the 9th and 11th century AD were not considered pirates but rather were called "Danes"or "Vikings". Another popular meaning of the word in medieval England was "sea thieves". The meaning of the word pirate most closely tied to the contemporary was established in the XVIII century AD. This definition dubbed pirates "outlaws" whom even persons who were not soldiers could kill. The first application of international law actually involved anti-pirate legislation. This is due to the fact that most pirate acts were committed outside the borders of any country.

Sometimes governments gave rights to the pirates to represent them in their wars. The most popular form was to give a license to a private sailor – privateer to attack enemy shipping on behalf of a specific king. Very often a privateer when caught by the enemy was tried as an outlaw notwithstanding the license.

The First New England Pirate

The very first pirate in the New World was Captain Dixie Bull who in 1632 began pirating, primarily in Penobscot Bay. Over the next few hundred years others would follow including William Kidd, Blackbeard, "Black" Sam Bellamy and others.

Pirate's Disability Pay

There is no argument that a pirate's job was indeed a hazardous one. To lose a limb, an eye or otherwise become disabled and, therefore no longer be an able bodied seaman, was a definite possibility. Some would claim they preferred a swift death over a debilitating disability. Compensation amounts by type of injuries are shown below. These were very sizable and generous amounts in the 1700s.

In pieces of eight

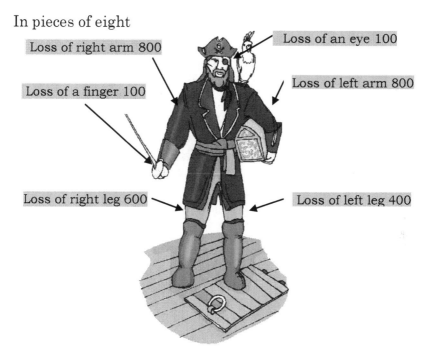

Loss of right arm 800

Loss of an eye 100

Loss of a finger 100

Loss of left arm 800

Loss of right leg 600

Loss of left leg 400

Disability payments would be made from the gross booty, and the individual shares would then be computed from the remainder. Injured pirates were given non-physically demanding work such as cooking meals, operating cannons, and washing the ship decks. They still were entitled to receive a normal share even though they were disabled and capable of limited participation.

Crew members that lost limbs in battle could be compensated at a rate of 800 pieces of eight per limb. Since infection could easily cause death, the remedy for gunshot wounds was often amputation.

With 100 men on a ship, if 10 limbs were lost during battle, that was 8,000 pieces of eight lost, or about $3.5 million in today's dollars. It's easy to see why pirates tried to take ships without firing a shot. A few drunken sailors getting wounded by sword or gunshot could negate the entire profit from a raid.

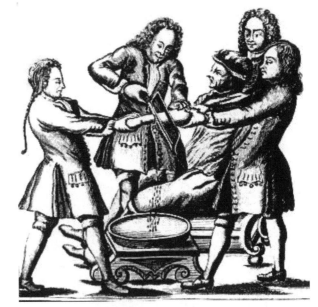

Pirate surgeon performing an amputation

Doctors aboard captured ships were often forced, against their will, by the pirates into service aboard the pirate's ship. Medicines were as prized by the pirates as was gold.

The Spanish Main

The New World coast from the top of South America through the Caribbean to Northern Florida was known as "The Spanish Main". It was from ports along these coasts that large Spanish treasure ships sailed for Europe and upon which pirates and privateers preyed. Outfitting warships ships was an expensive proposition for any government. In the 1700 and 1800s fleets of private ships were employed by governments to conduct war against their enemies as agents of the state.

Pirate Myths

Pirate Hooks:

Hooks were probably not as prevalent as one might imagine. Some attribute the popularity of pirates armed with hooks to the story "Peter Pan" that starred the pirate character Captain Hook.

Undoubtedly pirates did loose hands during their bloody battles. The few who might survive such a severe wound, given the level of medical prowess aboard the typical pirate ship, could have had such a device crafted by the ship's carpenter.

More likely he would bleed to death before the battle was over and medical attention rendered.

Parrots:

The genesis of the pirate and the parrot legend probably is the story "Treasure Island", specifically the character "Long John Silver". There is a good deal of debate on this subject as many expect that pirates were much too busy to permanently station a parrot upon their shoulder.

This legend becomes more unlikely when one realizes pirates at sea for long periods were more likely to prefer fresh meat over the companionship of a messy bird.

Peg Legs:

Popularity of this image probably originates from the story "Treasure Island", and the character "Long John Silver". Although there is basis for this image it is surely overdone.

When a pirate suffered a severe wound to the leg, as many were prone to do, the only option to save his life was amputation of the gangrened or infected limb. This job was usually given to either the ship's cook or carpenter as surgeons aboard pirate ships were uncommon.

As you might suspect few "operations" were successful. Those that did survive would, in addition to using crutches, often fashion a substitute limb out of available materials which most commonly was wood.

Eye Patch

Certainly a common injury to be sustained by pirates however, the only one of our pirates of the Golden Era known to wear an eye patch was Oliver La Buse.

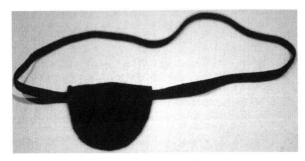

Eye Patch worn by pirates

Ships of the Era

Here is a sampling of ships on the seas during the Golden Age of Piracy :

Brig – Brigantine - a two masted ship, square rigged on both masts. The two ship types showed more variance in the 19th century. It was a popular choice of many pirate crews, carried as many as 10 cannon and had a crew of one hundred.

Frigate - name used for a variety of ships but formalized by the English in the late 17th century to mean a vessel smaller than a ship of the line. Carried 24-38 guns with three fully rigged masts, their speed made them well suited to convoy duty and hunting pirates.

Galleon - This was the ship of choice for the Spanish during the 16th through 18th centuries. It was 100-150 feet long, 40-50 feet wide and carried 600 tons or more. Usually had three masts and was square rigged with a lateen sail on the mizzenmast and two to three gun decks

Schooner: This 100 ton, with 8 cannon and a crew of 75 was a favorite amongst pirates because it was fast and shallow drafted. This meant they could easily catch slower moving cargo ships and, easily hide in shoal waters and coves to avoid capture by deep drafted "Man of Wars."

Sloop –Very popular with pirates because of its shallow draft and speed, capable of up to 11 knots, could carry up to 75 crew and mounted 14 cannon.

Naval Sloop: This was a pirate hunting ship. Armed with 12 nine pound cannons this 65 foot, 113 ton ship with a crew of 70 was dreaded by pirates. It was a very fast boat and the 7 pairs of oars allowed them to chase pirates even in windless conditions.

Merchant Ship: The name given to most commercial ships in the late 17th and early 18th centuries. This 80 foot, 280 ton ship manned by a crew of about 20 was referred to by seamen as a "Carrier." They were quite fast and could be armed with as many as 16 guns.

Dutch Flute: Very popular in the early 17th century as a cargo ship because this 300 ton, 80 foot ship was inexpensive to build and could be sailed with a crew of only 12. Because she carried half again as much cargo as similar ships, the Flute became the ship of choice of maritime interests and pirates alike.

Pirate Weapons

Cannon – Demi–cannon was a naval gun (French for half cannon) which fired a solid shot ranging in weight from 11lbs to 36lbs.

Cannon Shot – Cannons fired more than just cannon balls. Grape Shot - Iron balls, each the size of a tennis ball, bound in a canvas bag.

Chain Shot - Heavy balls joined by a chain designed to tangle and tear down rigging and masts

Canister Shot - Cylindrical cases containing pistol balls, used at close range to kill people

Carcass Shot – A flaming mistle filled with highly flammable matter, designed to set ships on fire.

Blunderbuss pistol - A short pistol of wide bore and flaring muzzle. It fires multiple balls at once. This made the blunderbuss the ideal weapon for boarding ships.

Other names for Pirate

Privateer - A ship privately owned and crewed but authorized by a government during wartime to attack and capture enemy vessels and accordingly, a privateer was supposedly not to be tried for piracy. Essentially a pirate was a self-employed soldier paid only by what he plundered from an enemy.

Buccaneer - The buccaneers were first hunters of pigs and cattle on the island of Hispaniola. They were driven off by the Spanish and turned to piracy therefore, the term originally referred to privateers who fought against the Spanish. Later it referenced sailors of the Atlantic, specifically the Caribbean. Buccaneers had a reputation of being heavy drinking, cruel sailors.

French settlers in the Caribbean who used to barbecue or "smoke" wild boar and oxen were called buccaneers. A *boucan* or *buccan* is the name for a wooden framework upon which meat would be smoked. Boucanier literally means "someone who makes smoke".

Marooners - Marooner is a corruption of the Spanish word "cimarrona" which loosely translates to "deserter" or runaway. These deserters or runaways fell into two groups:

- Spanish sailors who deserted their ship to escape the brutal treatment metered out by the Spanish navy and

- Cimmaron Negroes. These were the runaway of slaves that had been brought to the Americas by Spain to haul the gold

More names for a pirate:

Brethren of the Coast,
Brotherhood of the Coast,
On the Account,
Gentleman of Fortune,
Sea Dog,
Sailing with the Devil,
Freebooter,
Corsair,
Sea-wolf,
Sea-rover
Sailing under Articles

15

The Brass Monkey and Cold Weather Debate

The story: In the heyday of sailing ships, all war ships and many freighters carried iron cannons. Those cannons fired round iron cannon balls. It was necessary to keep a good supply near the cannon, but they had to find a way to prevent them from rolling about the deck.

The best storage method devised was a square based pyramid with one ball on top, resting on four resting on nine which rested on sixteen. Thus, a supply of 30 cannon balls could be stacked in a small area right next to the cannon.

There was only one problem; how to prevent the bottom layer from sliding or rolling from under the others. The solution was a metal plate called a "Monkey" with 16 round indentations. But, if this plate was made of iron, the iron balls quickly would rust to it. The solution to the rusting problem was to make "Brass Monkeys."

Few landlubbers realize that brass contracts much more and much faster than iron when chilled. Consequently, when the temperature dropped too far, the brass indentations would shrink so much that the iron cannon balls would come right off the monkey.

Thus, it was quite literally, "Cold enough to freeze the balls off a brass monkey." (And all this time, you thought that was an improper expression, didn't you?)

Rebuttal: This explanation appears to be a legend of the sea without historical justification. In actuality, ready service shot was kept on the gun or spar decks in shot racks (also known as shot garlands in the Royal Navy) which consisted of longitudinal wooden planks with holes bored into them, into which round shot (cannon balls) were inserted for ready use by the gun crew.

Pirate Flags

The ubiquitous skull and cross bones was not the flag flown by all pirate ships. In fact, most pirates developed their very own flag as sort of a trademark. They wanted to strike fear into the hearts of their prey by letting them know just who they were dealing with.

Flags flown by the more infamous pirates

Bartholomew Roberts (#1)

Bartholomew_Roberts (#2)

Christopher Moody

Edward England

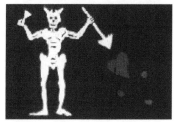
Edward Teach (Blackbeard)

Christopher Condent

Emanuel Wynne

Henry Every

Calico Jack Rackham

Richard Worley

Stede Bonnet

Thomas Tew

Walter Kennedy

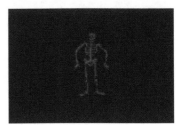

Edward Low

18

The Golden Age of Piracy Begins in Rhode Island

~

The Rogues of Rhode Island's Pirate Haven

Rhode Island, a Pirate's Haven

Piracy was a significant industry in Rhode Island and Newport a favorite refuge for pirates between voyages. Piracy was entrenched in Rhode Island from the mid 1600s through the early 1700s. In fact the other colonies would often refer to the state as "Rogues" Island.

A large number of pirates called Newport their home base. The problem the pirates presented was so severe that the London Board of Trade made an official complaint to the British government of the "great receptacle for pirates" at "Rode" Island.

In the 1690s, Newport was a major port in North America. Legal maritime activity was on the rise and increasingly rivaling piracy in economic importance. In 1695 and in response to the problem, the Earl of Bellomont financed an expedition by Captain Kidd against pirates "from New England, Rode Island, New York, and other parts in America".

Pirate Thomas Tew and New York's corrupt Governor conspire

The picture above is said to be of Rhode Island's notorious pirate Thomas Tew in conversation with New York's corrupt Governor Fletcher. Fletcher wrote in 1696 that "Rhode Island is now a free port for pirates. Thomas Tew brought there 100,000 pounds from the Red Sea in 1694."

In the 1720s under pressure from the British government, local officials decided they could no longer tolerate piracy. Legitimate commerce had overtaken piracy in economic importance and so the days of safe haven in Newport and environs came to an end. Many pirates were executed by hanging and buried on Goat Island in Newport Harbor.

Pirates, Privateers, & Smuggling

From 1650 until 1700, it could truly be said that piracy was an important industry in Rhode Island. Pirates fitted out in Rhode Island. Pirates obtained commissions in Rhode Island as a "privateer" that allowed them to capture the ships of an enemy, bring captured ships in Rhode Island and have the captured ship and contents legally declared property of the pirates (minus a percentage to the governor or government issuing the commission for someone to operate as a privateer).

A pirate bringing seized cargo ashore into Rhode Island was not paying custom taxes to England. To the English this was smuggling, avoiding payment of taxes. To the Rhode Islanders, this was simply part of everyday commerce, to pay pirates for goods at a cheaper price than otherwise available.

But cheaper goods was only part of a pirate's value to Rhode Island:

- For Rhode Island as a colony, getting a percentage "of the loot", was a government income without taxation of the local residents
- Privateering was a full employment policy for the colony: Rhode Islanders signed up as pirate crew members
- As a refuge and refitting base for pirates between voyages, Rhode Island was able to sell its own food, rum, lumber, goods, and shipbuilding repair services.

New Admiralty Court Established

Privateer Capt. John Hore was instrumental in Rhode Island establishing its own admiralty court -- outside of the Royal Admiralty Courts. In 1694, under a privateer's commission issued by English authority in Jamaica, Capt. Hore captured a fine French ship. He brought his prize back to Rhode Island -- instead of to New Providence in the Bahamas, because Rhode Island traditionally had not collected English customs taxes. Capt. Hore logically thought that by going to Rhode Island he would be able to avoid paying the English customs taxes, plus avoid paying the percentage due the British government in Jamaica.

21

However, upon arrival in Newport, Rhode Island Capt. Hore was dismayed to find there was at that time no Admiralty Court in Rhode Island to declare the property was legally his. Capt. Hore petitioned the governor of Rhode Island to establish an Admiralty Court. The governor complied declaring he thought it his patriotic duty, as an Englishman, to encourage attacks against the French, and Rhode Island quickly established an Admiralty Court. The newly established Court duly declared the captured French ship and her cargo legally that of Capt. Hore.

Capt. Hore settled in as a resident of Rhode Island for the winter, had the Rhode Island shipbuilders fit out his captured ship as a "privateer" and sailed off the next year to the Pacific's East Indies to be a pirate in that area.

Off to Rob, Pillage and Burn

"Privateer" Captain Colly was a Rhode Island pirate who brought in the *Pelican* a ship sized from the French. It was quickly refitted with 16 guns, and a crew of 100. Rhode Island Governor Walter Clares issued a customs clearance to have the *Pelican* sail to return a number of sailors captured on the *Pelican* to Jamaica.

Apparently many persons knew that Capt Colly and his crew intended "to cruise on the Moors, not intending to Pirate among the Europeans, but honestly and quietly to rob what Moors fell in their way."

Captain, Colly, promptly engaged and paid the Deputy Collector of Customs, Gardiner, to be his attorney and to take care of business for him while he was gone from Rhode Island, and Gardiner promptly cleared the ship for sailing from Rhode Island to Jamaica.

Capt Colly cruised off to Madagascar and is reported to have proceeded to do the "usual rob, pillage and burn" of settlements on islands near Madagascar.

Newport Justice

The trial of Pirate George Cutler illustrated how the legal system of Rhode Island was used as a refuge for pirates and to obtain the equivalent of what we today call "money laundering".

In 1698, Cutler was arrested for piracy and having a large sum of money in his possession which he had in his ship *Fowy*. He was immediately let out on bail, awaiting a trial. The rules of the trial were that if no one physically showed up to claim he was the owner of the cash and goods, the prisoner was acquitted and the court would declare the accused to be the rightful owner of the goods.

Cutler was tried before the Court of General Tryalls at Newport on the charge of piracy. No one offered any proof against him. Questioned where he had got the money, Cutler said it got it in various places, included being willed some of it by a resident of Madagascar. The jury acquitted; and Cutler took up residency in Newport, Rhode Island, with his stash of cash.

Usually, if a trial as to whether the accused was a pirate with stolen goods in his possession was not expected to clear the person accused of piracy, the prisoner took advantage of a wonderfully negligent succession of sheriffs and jailers. E.g., William Downs escaped from Jail in April 1698, it was duly reported that the Under Sheriff let Downs out of jail to "ease himself". No sheriff or undersheriff was ever tried for any crime or negligence.

Richest Piracy in History plotted at Newport's White Horse Tavern?

Was the White Horse Tavern the pirate's safe haven in Newport and where the plot to plunder the richest treasure of all time was hatched? Pirating by New England pirates was not restricted to America's east coast and the Caribbean; in fact New England pirates were to be found in every ocean and sea around the world. Birds of a feather flock together so, as one would expect, after returning to Newport the pirates would meet, perhaps at the White Horse Tavern, and swap tales of their adventures in far away waters. One can imagine pirate captains Joseph Farrell, William May and Thomas Tew swapping tales of their adventures, each attempting to better the stories of the other

Their tales would naturally progress to those of the richest "hunting ground" of the world. They would describe the unimaginable riches the richest persons on earth would transport across the seas once every year. The progression would lead these three men and two other pirate captains, William Want of Philadelphia and Captain Wake of Boston, to sail half way around the world into the Indian Ocean and the Red Sea in search of fantastic treasure.

White Horse Tavern

Once there they would meet up with the notorious pirate H*enry Every* and elect Every fleet captain and lead the capture of the largest treasure ship in history

The Target

The Great Moghul of India Richest Man on Earth

Aurangzeb, aka Alamgir I (1618 – 1707). He was the last of the great Mughal emperors of India. He was the son of Shah Jahan and Mumtaz Mahal, for whom the Taj Mahal was built.

Aurangzeb

He was Muslim monarch of a mixed Hindu-Muslim empire. He is reported to have executed the Sikh Guru Tegh Bahadur thereby starting a Sikh-Muslim feud that has continued to the present.

He ruled India for 48 years expanding the Mughal Empire to its greatest extent, encompassing all but the southern tip of the Indian subcontinent. He remains one of the most controversial figures in Indian history. His successors, the 'Later Mughals', lacked his strong hand and the Hindu Maratha Empire mostly replaced Mughal rule during the rest of the 18th century.

The Badshahi Mosque (King's mosque) was completed in 1675 by the Mughal emperor Aurangzeb. It is large enough to accommodate more than 55,000 worshippers and is the second largest mosque in India

25

The Pirate Fleet Assembles

In 1695, off Perim Island in the Red Sea, six pirate ships assembled in preparation for raiding pilgrims sailing from Mecca to India. The Newport pirates had elected Captain "Long Ben" Every aboard his ship the 46 gun *Fancy* as fleet captain and they were itching to plunder.

In the fleet was Thomas Tew, a native Rhode Islander aboard his ship *Dolphin*. Tew had retired after returning a rich man from his previous pirating tour but apparently, the lure of additional riches and adventure were too much to resist.

Tew would sail to the Red Sea in consort with captains William Want from Philadelphia and his ship *Dolphin* and Thomas Wake of Boston on the *Susanna* reaching the Red Sea in June of 1695. Captain William May aboard the *Pearl* and the *Portsmouth Adventurer* captained by Joseph Farrell joined them there also.

Pirate Ships sail to Red Sea

This fleet of six well-armed pirate ships were now powerful enough to attack the heavily armored and protected treasure ships that plied the routes to and from Mecca. The pirates sighted two ships. The smaller of the two was the unarmed merchant ship *Fateh Mahmamadi*, carrying gold and silver valued at more than £50,000.

The second ship was the *Gang-i-Sawai*, one of the Great Moghul's largest ships bristling with an estimated eighty great guns and five hundred musketeers. Although outgunned the pirates did not hesitate to attack.

The Biggest Prize in History

Gold, Silver, Diamonds and 100 Virgins

Two lucky shots turned the tide in favor of the pirates. The first caused an explosion on the main deck killing the captain and the second dropped the mainmast hindering the ship's ability to manuever. In the ensuring two hour battle the now leaderless crew aboard their crippled ship finally surrendered to the pirates. The Gang-i-Sawai turned out to be the mother of all treasure ships.

Pirates do battle

Aboard the ship, the pirates would find treasure in gold, silver and diamonds estimated to be worth $188,000,000 in 2,000 AD dollars. Each sailor's full share would be worth $3,500,000 today.

Boys under 18 would receive an amount in excess of a sailor of the day's lifetime earnings. According to all accounts, this was the greatest robbery of all time.

A daughter of the Great Moghul is reported to have been among the six hundred captured passengers that included more than one hundred beautiful virgins ages 12 to 18. They had been handpicked as additions to the Grand Mogul's harem. Captain Every claimed no harm befell the women. However, one pirate later confessed at his trial that the pirates committed "horrid barbarities."

When the Great Moghul learned of the attack, he vented his outrage on the English and the East India Company, threatening to force the English out of India. Assurances that the pirates would be brought to justice and heavy negotiations eventually calmed the Grand Moguls wrath.

Thomas Tew

Native Rhode Island Pirate

Gravelly Thomas Tew, born in Newport, Rhode Island, was one
of the first pirates to
successfully sail the
Pirate Round around the
Cape of Good Hope into
the Indian Ocean and
plunder the treasure ships
of the Great Mogul of
India.

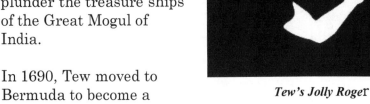

Tew's Jolly Roger

In 1690, Tew moved to
Bermuda to become a
privateer. With a
commission from Bermuda's Governor Isaac Richier, he set sail
to take a French factory on the Gambia River in Africa. But
once at sea, Tew told his crew that there was little to be gained
in Africa and great danger in gaining it.

Instead, he offered them a much more lucrative choice: sail to
the Red Sea and plunder the treasure-laden ships of the Great
Mogul of India. The proposition was greeted with great cheers
and the unified cry, "A gold chain or a wooden leg, we'll stand
by you!"

Captain Tew and his pirate crew of forty, emboldened by their
new commitment, had the audacity to attack a huge, heavily
armed Mogul treasure ship laden with gold, silver, pearls,
gems, spices, ivory, and silk. After a brief battle, the 300
turban-clad Indian soldiers dropped their muskets and
scimitars and fell to their knees in surrender.

No one in Tew's crew was injured. Tew sailed his eight-gun ship
Amity to the tiny island of St. Mary's off the coast of
Madagascar where the crew careened the ship, restocked
supplies, and divided the plunder. Every man received 3,000
pounds sterling ($3.5 million by today's standards) with a
double share for Captain Tew. It was an amazing amount of
wealth.

When Tew returned to Rhode Island after his adventure, he was welcomed as a conquering hero and invited to dine with the most prestigious families. Tew, his wife, and two daughters were honored as the special guests of Governor Fletcher of New

Tew and the Governor

York. Every colonial wanted to see Tew's riches and hear his tales of Arabia.

In 1694, Tew embarked on another voyage, promising his family it would be his last. Unfortunately, it was. Roving once again in the Red Sea, his sloop was one of a squadron of six pirate ships led by Henry Every attempting to overpower a fleet of Mogul ships. This time his rich dreams were not to become reality.

In September 1695, Tew met his gory demise during the very first exchange of broadsides with the Mogul ships' great guns. His stomach was torn away with a cannon ball and he was said to be holding his bowels in his hands as he hit the quarterdeck. With their famous captain dead, the crew panicked and surrendered their fate to the enemy.

Henry Every, Disappeared 1696

Made only one voyage as a pirate but scored the Richest Prize in History

Henry Every or Avery was a pirate whose aliases included John

Avary, Long Ben, and Benjamin Bridgeman. He is most famous for being apparently one of the few major pirate captains to retire with his loot without being arrested or killed in battle.

Every's Jolly Roger

Every was a sailor from youth, serving on

various Royal Navy ships. Some accounts place him aboard the English fleet bombarding Algiers in 1671, buccaneering in the Caribbean Sea, and captaining a logwood freighter. By the early 1690s he had entered the Atlantic slave trade, in which he was known to buy slaves on the West African coast, then seize the slave traders themselves and chain them in his ship's hold alongside their former captives.

Every only made one voyage in his capacity as a pirate captain. But in that single journey he said to have succeeded in committing, as "the single richest crime in history." In August, 1694, Every and his ship, the *Fancy*, reached the Mandab Strait, where he teamed up with four other pirate ships, including Thomas Tew's sloop *Amity*. Every and his men attacked the Fateh Muhammed, which had earlier repulsed an attack by the *Amity*, killing Captain Tew. Perhaps intimidated by the *Fancy's* 46 guns or weakened by their earlier battle with Tew, the Fateh Muhammed's crew put up little resistance, and Every's pirates sacked the ship for £50,000 worth of treasure.

Every then sailed in pursuit of the *Ganj-I-Sawai*, overtaking her about eight days out of Surat. After a violent battle, Every took the ship. The loot from the *Ganj-I-Sawai* totalled between £325,000 and £600,000, including 500,000 gold and silver pieces.

Unable to buy a pardon from the governor of Jamaica, Every's crew split up, some heading to New England, while the majority, including Every, returned to Britain aboard the sloop *Isaac,* landing in Ireland. Although 24 of his men were caught, many soon after disembarking, Every was never seen again. His last words to his men were a litany of conflicting stories of where he planned to go, doubtless intended to throw pursuers off his trail.

Persian Gold Coins circa 1694-1722

Britain Moves Against Pirates

The seizure of the Grand Mogul's treasure ships brought the "Piracy Issue" to a head in England. English officials were not only criticizing Rhode Island for failing to observe the customs laws, but also for serving as a base for pirates which were causing the crown much embarrassment and financial trouble.

The commission to investigate the situation reported 25 paragraphs of irregularities. Among these were the issuance by Deputy Governor Green of commissions to persons who thereupon committed piracy in the seas of India and the "coutenancing and harbouring of pirates".

Naturally, the finding by the English Board of Trade so shocked the Rhode Island government that it promised reform, and therfore the King took no action.

Captain Kidd to the Rescue

In response to the piratical activities emanating in New England, the Earl of Bellomont financed an expedition by Captain Kidd against pirates "from New England, Rode Island, New York, and other parts in America".

Two years later, in August of 1697, the English Board of Trade was referring to Rhode Island as "having become a great receptacle for pirates" By December 1698 the Board recommended to the King the issuance of a "writ of quo warranto" for removal of the Rhode Island charter.

It may not have been so much the pressure from England's Board of Trade that caused the general attitude of Rhode Islanders against pirates. After 1700 Rhode Island was the base for increasing numbers of merchant ships, and Rhode Island's merchant ships were distressingly more often captured by pirates. The Rhode Island attitude and actions soon became one of intolerance to pirates *based outside of Rhode Island* (but not of Rhode Island colonists who went out of Rhode Island harbors on pirate missions).

Pirates Executed

Contemporaneous account of the proceedings

Two pirate sloops, the *Ranger*, and the *Fortune*, which had committed various piracies on the high seas, being in company, on the 8th May, 1723, captured the ship *Amsterdam Merchant*, John Welland, master; the day after which capture they plundered and sunk the ship.

On the 6th day of June in lat. 39, they took a Virginia sloop, rifled her, and let her go, who the next day fell in with His Majesty's Ship, the *Greyhound*, Capt. Solgard, of 20 guns, to whom they related the circumstances of their late capture and release. Capt. Solgard immediately pursued, and on the 10th, came up with the pirate sloops, about 14 leagues south of the east end of Long Island, who, mistaking him for a merchant ship, immediately gave chase, and soon commenced firing on the *Greyhound*, under a black flag, but then hauled down the black flag and hoisted a red one.

The *Greyhound* succeeded in capturing one of the sloops, after having seven men wounded, but the other pirate escaped. The *Greyhound* came with the prize into the harbor of Newport, and the pirates, thirty-six in number, were committed for trial; twenty-six were sentenced to be hanged, which execution took place on Gravelly Point, opposite the town, on the 19th July, 1723. After execution, their bodies were carried to Goat Island and buried on the shore, between high and low water mark.

The Salem Observer, November 11, 1843:

> *"...this was the most extensive execution of pirates that ever took place at one time in the Colonies, it was attended by a vast multitude from every part of New England."*

Pirates Last Roll Call

The names and ages of the pirates that were executed on Friday, July the 19th, 1723 at Newport, Rhode Island are listed below.

Most of these men were foreigners; but one belonged to Rhode Island. They were principally natives of England. There never was a greater number executed at any one period, in the history of this county.

NAME	AGE	OCCUPATION	CRIME	METHOD	DATE
BLADES, WILLIAM	28	SEAMAN	PIRACY	HANGING	JUL 19 1723
HARRIS, CHARLES		SHIP CAPTAIN	PIRACY	HANGING	JUL 19 1723
HUGGET, THOMAS	24	SEAMAN	PIRACY	HANGING	JUL 19 1723
LINNICAR, THOMAS	21	SEAMAN	PIRACY	HANGING	JUL 19 1723
CUES, PETER	32	SEAMAN	PIRACY	HANGING	JUL 19 1723
HYDE, DANIEL	23	SEAMAN	PIRACY	HANGING	JUL 19 1723
JONES, WILLIAM	28	SEAMAN	PIRACY	HANGING	JUL 19 1723
MUNDON, STEPHEN	29	SEAMAN	PIRACY	HANGING	JUL 19 1723
EATON, EDWARD	38	SEAMAN	PIRACY	HANGING	JUL 19 1723
LACY, ABRAHAM	21	SEAMAN	PIRACY	HANGING	JUL 19 1723
BROWN, JOHN	29	SEAMAN	PIRACY	HANGING	JUL 19 1723
LAWSON, EDWARD	20	SEAMAN	PIRACY	HANGING	JUL 19 1723
SPRINKLEY, JAMES	28	SEAMAN	PIRACY	HANGING	JUL 19 1723
TOMKINS, JOHN	21	SEAMAN	PIRACY	HANGING	JUL 19 1723
SOUND, JOSEPH	28	SEAMAN	PIRACY	HANGING	JUL 19 1723
LAUGHTON, FRANCIS	39	SEAMAN	PIRACY	HANGING	JUL 19 1723
CHURCH, CHARLES	21	SEAMAN	PIRACY	HANGING	JUL 19 1723
FITZGERALD, JOHN	21	SEAMAN	PIRACY	HANGING	JUL 19 1723
STUTFIELD, WILLIAM	40	SEAMAN	PIRACY	HANGING	JUL 19 1723
RICE, OWEN	27	SEAMAN	PIRACY	HANGING	JUL 19 1723
RHAD, WILLIAM	35	SEAMAN	PIRACY	HANGING	JUL 19 1723
HAZEL, THOMAS		SEAMAN	PIRACY	HANGING	JUL 19 1723
BRIGHT, JOHN		SEAMAN	PIRACY	HANGING	JUL 19 1723
LIBBEY, JOSEPH		SEAMAN	PIRACY	HANGING	JUL 19 1723
POWEST, THOMAS	21	SEAMAN	PIRACY	HANGING	JUL 19 1723
WATERS, JOHN	35	SEAMAN	PIRACY	HANGING	JUL 19 1723

The
Golden Age
of Piracy

and
New Providence

The Golden Age of Piracy

Our pirates ruled the Caribbean during the "Golden Age" of Piracy, which lasted roughly from 1690 to 1730. Some historians vary on the definition of the Golden Age of Piracy with the broadest accepted definition range from the 1650s to the 1730s.

During this Golden Age of Piracy, privateers, buccaneers, and pirates attacked shipping lanes and seaborne trade occurring predominately throughout the Caribbean waters, the Atlantic seaboard of America, the West African coast, and the Indian Ocean.

What Factors Brought About the Golden Age of Piracy?

- Wars
- Letters of Marque
- The Spanish Gold Fleet
- Value of the Cargos
- Spain's Naval Forces Depleted
- Hurricane Sinks Treasure Fleet of 1715
- Poor Economy and Lack of Work

Wars - The Golden Age of Piracy emerged as a result of what might be thought of as a World War. In Europe, the major powers were busy fighting each other in the *War of the Spanish Succession* (1701–1714).

This war was fought between European powers, including a divided Spain, over who had the right to succeed Charles II as King of Spain. The war was fought mostly in Europe and essentially all of the major powers of Europe were heavily engaged in this major and history making struggle. As a result, the piratical activities in the Americas became merely a distraction and therefore overlooked by the European powers allowing piracy to flourish unimpeded by authorities and law.

The raging war in Europe combined with a weak colonial government made the Americans a preferred hunting ground for pirates.

Meanwhile in North America, *Queen Anne's War* (1702 – 1713) the North American theater of the *War of the Spanish Succession,* was raging. This was one in a series of French and Indian Wars fought between France and England in North America for control of the North American continent.

This war involved numerous Native American tribes allied with each nation, and Spain, which was allied with France. It was also known as the Third Indian War.

The war concluded with the Peace of Utrecht (1713), in which the warring states recognized the French candidate as King Philip V of Spain in exchange for territorial and economic concessions.

Letters of Marque –

In times of war governments would use *letters of marque and reprisal* as a means of augmenting their fighting forces. It was a government license issued to private citizens authorizing their attack, plunder and capture of enemy vessels.

Letter de Marque

A letter of marque and reprisal in effect converted a private merchant vessel into a naval auxiliary. A commissioned privateer enjoyed the protection of the laws of war. If captured, the crew was entitled to honorable treatment as prisoners of war, while without the license they were deemed mere pirates "at war with all the world," and mere criminals who were properly hanged.

Cruising for prizes with a *letter of marque* was considered an honorable calling combining patriotism and profit, in contrast to <u>unlicensed</u> piracy, which was universally condemned. The *letters of marque* introduced thousands of seamen to pirating via privateering.

Spanish Gold Fleet

For 300 years Spain had been transporting Silver, Gold and other treasures back to Spain in large convoys of treasure galleons. This activity was a natural attraction to those seeking adventure as well as fortune. Wars with Spain and the resulting privateers led to a large number of experienced privateers (pirates) plying America's waters.

Value of the Cargo

A Peso or Piece of Eight had about 25 grams of silver, about the same as the US Silver dollar. A single galleon might carry 2 million pesos.

At the time of this writing silver was selling for about $20 an ounce. Simple math calculates the typical value of the cargo of a Spanish galleon to approximate $40,000,000 in today's dollars.

Value of Silver

Spain's Naval Forces Depleted

The Spanish treasure fleet of 1702 was destroyed in the *Battle of Vigo Bay* on Spain's Iberian Peninsula during the *War of the Spanish Succession*. The fleet was surprised at port while unloading its treasure.

France was providing escort protection for this treasure fleet and lost all of her war ships in this battle thereby leaving Spain's Naval forces drastically reduced and effectively causing Spain's interests in the Caribbean to become unprotected. Good news for the pirates and their numbers continued to increase unopposed.

Hurricane Sinks Treasure Fleet of 1715

Treasure ship flounders before sinking

Spain's Treasure Fleet of 1715 was returning to Spain when on the evening of July 30, seven days after departing from Havana, Cuba, eleven of the twelve ships of this fleet were lost in a hurricane near present day Vero Beach, Florida. Some artifacts and even coins still can be found on the Vero Beach sands from time to time.

An estimated 1,000 sailors perished while a small number were able to make it to shore and survive. Over time, many ships, including pirate ships, were to take part in salvage efforts.

It was the stories of this massive sinking of treasure that motivated the young Samuel Bellamy, who was serving under Captain Henry Jennings as a privateer, to leave his wife and family in England and come to the Colonies and find some of this treasure for his own.

The pirate Charles Vane, while in the Bahamas serving under pirate Captain Henry Jennings, heard of this Spanish treasure fleet that dumped tons of Spanish gold and silver not far from shore. They were close by and immediately made way to the wreck site. The surviving Spanish sailors were still salvaging what they could from the sunken galleons as Jennings and Vane were making a beeline for the treasure site.

They were the first ship to reach it and, instead of diving into the waters to join in with the salvaging of the treasure, the buccaneers chose to raid the Spanish camp on shore instead, making off with some £87,000 in recovered gold and silver.

Satisfied with what they had plundered from the surviving Spanish sailors they left the scene before more ships and possible trouble could arrive.

Poor Economy and Lack of Work - The attractiveness of piracy increased during this period due to: the end of a long war, ports full of unemployed sailors, and lack of legal employment.

Most pirates were English (35%), but other nationalities were also represented: colonials from America-25%, colonials from the West Indies-20%, Scots-10%, Welsh-8%, and Swedish/Dutch/French/Spanish-2%. A fair number of blacks also joined the pirates. When Black Bart Roberts was captured, 75 blacks served amongst his crew of 228 men.

Benefits of Becoming a Pirate

Sailors of the day were routinely underpaid or even cheated of their wages completely. The ships were often filthy or unsafe and the officers were unduly strict and harsh.

Many were pressed into service against their will. Navy "press gangs" roamed the streets when sailors were needed, beating able-bodied men into unconsciousness and securing them on board ship until it sailed.

Life as a pirate could be a more attractive alternative to many of the sailors of the day. Serving aboard a pirate ship was more civil and democratic plus: it was extremely more profitable. Pirates were diligent about sharing the loot fairly, and punishments were rarely needless or capricious. In the words of "Black Bart" Roberts:

> *"In an honest service there is thin commons, low wages, and hard labor; in this, plenty and satiety, pleasure and ease, liberty and power; and who would not balance creditor on this side, when all the hazard that is run for it, at worst, is only a sour look or two at choking.*
>
> *No, a merry life and a short one, shall be my motto."*

Bartholomew "Black Bart" Robert's slogan and flag

Pirates Create Their Own Republic

With the Help of a Corrupt Governor

Lord Archibald Hamilton was a Royal Navy officer and British politician. He became a Captain in the Royal Navy and in 1714 and was appointed Governor of Jamaica by King George.

He played a controversial role in setting up some of the founders of the infamous "Flying Gang", including Henry Jennings, Charles Vane and Blackbeard for which he was arrested and brought back to England by the Royal Navy only to be subsequently released.

He oversaw and did not oppose the establishment of the Pirate Republic at New Providence. It was from this safe haven that pirates of the Golden Age would operate with impunity.

New Providence, Pirate's Haven

The island of New Providence is in the Bahamas, in the Atlantic Ocean close to the Caribbean Sea and about two thousand miles from Cape Cod.

In 1704, the island of New Providence was abandoned as an English colony because of its susceptibility to Spanish and French attacks. Between 1700 and 1718, New Providence became a favorite harbor with pirate and the home of the notorious "Flying Gang" of pirates.

It is reported that Edward Teach (Blackbeard) and "Black Sam" Bellamy of Whydah Gally fame, banded together to form a pirate cooperative which eventually became the "Pirate Republic." It was a very democratic form of governing in which blacks were equal citizens and sailors would choose their Captain by vote. For a brief, glorious period they were astoundingly successful, and so disruptive to shipping that the governors of Jamaica, Virginia, Bermuda, and the Carolinas all began clamoring for something to be done.

Much of the pirates and the Flying Gang's success was due, in part, to their establishing the Pirate Republic at New Providence as it provided them with a fortified base from which they could not be easily dislodged.

By 1714, more than 500 pirates had complete control over New Providence and its port. The port had several features that were beneficial to the pirates.

- The pirate ships could navigate its shallow waters. However, the larger, deeper drafted Man of War ships could not thereby preventing them from attacking the pirates in the harbor.

- The island provided an abundant supply of food, water, timber and other necessities for the pirates and their ships.

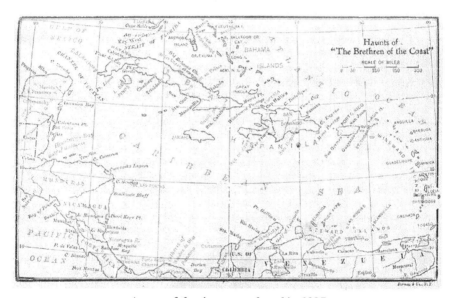

A map of the time reproduced in 1897

- New Providence's close proximity to trade routes allowed for a continuous stream of ships to pass close by and be plundered by the pirates.

43

The Golden Age Begins to Tarnish

Just as factors combined to facilitate the birth of the Golden Age of Piracy, other factors began to combine to bring about its end.

- Strategy change by Spain
- War in Europe ends
- King degrees "Piracy must end"
- Royal pardons offered
- New governor and armed fleet arrive

Change of Strategy

When Spain realized she could do little to diminish the growing number of the pirate vessels a decision was made to change the way valuable cargos from the Americas would be shipped back to Spain. This one change would have a dramatic impact on the pirates in the Caribbean and make piracy along the Atlantic, including New England, coast an attractive alternative.

The relatively small cargo carrying Galleons would be replaced by much larger and heavily armed ships of war. The cargoes of three galleons could be crowded into the holds and between the decks of just one of these great vessels. Being so well armed and defended it was almost impossible for any pirate ship to capture it.

However, when pirates were able to attack swiftly and in significant numbers, they sometimes were able to capture a prize far more valuable than anyone could have imagined before.

The End of War in Europe

In 1713, the Treaty of Utrecht ended war between the European nations and the several European states' ability to police piracy was massively increased. Now European naval ships could concentrate on hunting down those troublesome pirates.

The pirates had been able to prosper in the power vacuum the period of upheaval and war had created. Governments were preoccupied with the war and that allowed the pirates freedom

44

to operate unopposed outside the law. With the coming of peace came an end to the continuation of pirate autonomy.

King Degrees Piracy Must End

1717 England decided to put an end to the pirate plague. Royal Navy ships were sent and many pirate hunters were commissioned. Woodes Rogers, a tough former privateer, was made governor of Jamaica. His main charge was to stamp out piracy.

Royal Pardon Sped the Demise

A Royal Pardon however, would prove to be the most effective tool to eliminate piracy. A royal pardon was offered by King George I of England for pirates who wanted out of the life and Woodes Rogers appointed governor to eradicate piracy. Many pirates took it.

Some, like Benjamin Hornigold, stayed legit, while others who took the pardon, like Blackbeard or Charles Vane, soon returned to piracy. Although piracy would continue, slowly, judicial and naval pressure put an end to piratical activities in the

King George I

Americas, and by 1730, it was all but over.

Woodes Rogers

Sent to New Providence to end Piracy

Rogers was an English sea captain, privateer, and, later, the first Royal Governor of the Bahamas. He is known as the captain of the vessel that rescued the marooned Alexander Selkirk, whose plight is generally believed to have inspired Daniel Defoe's *Robinson Crusoe*.

His Background

Rogers came from an affluent seafaring family, grew up in Poole and Bristol, and served a marine apprenticeship to a Bristol sea captain. His father, who held shares in many ships, died when Rogers was in his mid-twenties, leaving Rogers in control of the family shipping business.

He turns to Privateering to solve financial problems, Rescues *"Robinson Crusoe"*

In 1707, Rogers began privateering against the Spanish, with whom the British were at war in order to recoup financial losses. Rogers led the expedition, which consisted of two well-armed ships, the *Duke* and the *Duchess*, and was the captain of the *Duke*. In three years, Rogers and his men went around the world, capturing several ships in the Pacific Ocean. En route, the expedition rescued *"Robinson Crusoe"* from Juan Fernandez Island on February 1, 1709. When the expedition returned to England in October 1711,

Robinson Crusoe

Rogers had circumnavigated the globe, while retaining his original ships and most of his men, and the investors in the expedition doubled their money.

Rogers was the first Englishman, in circumnavigating the globe, to have his original ships and most of his crew survive.

While the expedition made Rogers a national hero, his brother was killed and Rogers was badly wounded in fights in the Pacific. Rogers encountered financial problems on his return. His influential father-in-law, Sir William Whetstone, had died, and Rogers, having failed to recoup his business losses through privateering, was forced to sell his Bristol home to support his family.

He was successfully sued by a group of over 200 of his crew, who stated that they had not received their fair share of the expedition profits.

The profits from his book were not enough to overcome these setbacks, and he was forced into bankruptcy. His wife gave birth to

Rogers sued by his crew

their fourth child a year after his return, a boy who died in infancy, and Woodes and Sarah Rogers soon permanently separated.

Roger's connections with several of the advisers to the new king, George I, who had succeeded Queen Anne in 1714, enabled Rogers to forge an agreement for a company to manage the pirate infested Bahamas in exchange for a share of the colony's profits.

Clemency for Pirates Proclaimed

On January 5, 1718, a proclamation was issued announcing clemency for all piratical offences, provided that those seeking what became known as the "King's Pardon" surrendered not later than September 5, 1718. Colonial governors and deputy governors were authorized to grant the pardon.

Rogers was officially appointed "Captain General and Governor in Chief" by George I on January 6, 1718. He did not leave immediately for his new bailiwick, but spent several months preparing the expedition, which included seven ships, 100 soldiers, 130 colonists, and supplies ranging from food for the expedition members and ships' crews to religious pamphlets to give to the pirates, whom Rogers believed would respond to spiritual teachings. On April 22, 1718, the expedition, accompanied by three Royal Navy vessels, sailed out of the Thames.

The expedition arrived on July 22, 1718, surprising and trapping a ship commanded by pirate Charles Vane. After negotiations failed, Vane used a captured French vessel as a fireship in an attempt to ram the naval vessels. The attempt failed, but the naval vessels were forced out of the west end of Nassau harbor, giving Vane's crew an opportunity to raid the town and secure the best local pilot. Vane and his men then escaped in a small sloop via the harbor's narrow east entrance. The pirates had evaded the trap, but Nassau and New Providence Island were in Rogers' hands.

Expedition arrives at New Providence

At the time, the island's population consisted of about two hundred former pirates and several hundred fugitives who had escaped from nearby Spanish colonies. Rogers organized a government, granted the King's Pardon to those former pirates on the island who had not yet accepted it, and started to rebuild the island's fortifications, which had fallen into decrepitude under pirate domination.

Faces a Double Threat from Pirates and Loss of Half his Contingent to Disease

However, less than a month into his residence on New Providence, Rogers was faced with a double threat: Vane wrote, threatening to join with Edward Teach (better known as Blackbeard) to retake the island and Rogers learned that the Spanish also planned to drive the British out of the Bahamas.

Rogers' expedition suffered further setbacks. An unidentified disease killed almost a hundred of his expedition members, while leaving the long-term residents nearly untouched.

His Naval Escorts Leave

Two of the three navy vessels, having no orders to remain, left for New York. Ships sent to Havana to conciliate the Spanish governor there never arrived, their crew revolting and becoming pirates mid-voyage. Finally, the third naval vessel left in mid-September, its commander promising to return in three weeks, a promise he had no intention of keeping. Work on rebuilding the island's fortifications proceeded slowly, with the locals showing a disinclination to work.

Disease disseminates expedition

On September 14, 1718, Rogers received word that Vane was at Green Turtle Cay near Abaco, about 120 miles north of Nassau. Some of the pardoned pirates on New Providence took boats to join Vane, and Rogers decided to send two ex-pirate captains, Benjamin Hornigold and John Cockram, with a crew to gather intelligence, and, if possible, to bring Vane to battle.

As the weeks passed, and hope of their return dimmed, Rogers declared martial law and set all inhabitants to work on rebuilding the island's fortifications. Finally, the former pirates returned. They had failed to find an opportunity to kill Vane or bring him to battle, but had captured one ship and a number of pirate captives.

Captain Hornigold was then sent to recapture the ships and crews who had gone pirate en route to Havana. He returned with ten prisoners and three corpses. On December 9, 1718, Rogers brought the ten men captured by Hornigold to trial. Nine were convicted, and Rogers had eight hanged three days later, reprieving the ninth on hearing he was of good family.

One of the condemned, Thomas Morris, quipped as he climbed the gallows, "We have a good governor, but a harsh one." The executions so cowed the populace that when, shortly after Christmas, several residents plotted to overthrow Rogers and restore the island to piracy, the conspirators attracted little support. Rogers had them flogged, then released as harmless.

Pirate hung from the gallows

On March 16, 1719 Rogers learned that Spain and Britain were at war again. He redoubled his efforts to repair the island's fortifications, buying vital supplies on credit in the hope of later being reimbursed by the expedition's investors. The Spanish sent an invasion fleet against Nassau in May, but when the fleet's commodore learned that the French (now Britain's ally) had captured Pensacola, he directed the fleet there instead. This gave Rogers time to continue to fortify and supply New Providence, and it was not until February 24, 1720 that a Spanish fleet arrived. Wary of Rogers' defenses, the Spanish landed troops on Paradise Island (then known as Hog Island), which shelters Nassau's harbor. They were driven off by Rogers' troops.

The year 1720 brought an end to external threats to Rogers' rule. With Spain and Britain at peace again, the Spanish made no further move against the Bahamas. Vane never returned, having been shipwrecked and captured in the Bay Islands. A year later, he was hanged in Jamaica.

This did not end Rogers' problems as governor. Overextended from financing New Providence's defenses, he received no assistance from Britain, and merchants refused to give him further credit. His health suffered, and he spent six weeks in Charleston, South Carolina, hoping to recuperate. Instead, he was wounded in a duel with Captain John Hildesley of HMS *Flamborough*, a duel caused by disputes between the two on New Providence. Troubled by the lack of support and communication from London, Rogers set sail for Britain in March 1721. He arrived three months later to find that a new governor had been appointed, and his company had been liquidated. Personally liable for the obligations he had contracted at Nassau, he was imprisoned for debt.

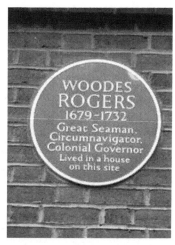

Plaque on the site of Rogers' Bristol residence

With both the government and his former partners refusing to honor his debts, Rogers was released from debtor's prison only when his creditors took pity on him and absolved him of his debts. Even so, Rogers wrote that he was "perplexed with the melancholy prospect of [his] affairs". In 1722 or 1723, Rogers was approached by a man writing a history of piracy, and supplied him with information. The resulting work, *A General History of the Robberies and Murders of the Most Notorious Pyrates*, published under the pseudonym Captain Charles Johnson, was an enormous hit on both sides of the Atlantic, and catapulted Rogers for the second time to the status of a national hero.

With public attention focused on him again, Rogers was successful in 1726 in petitioning the king for financial redress. Not only did King George I grant him a pension, retroactive to 1721, but the king's son and successor, George II, reappointed him as governor on October 22, 1728.

The Bahamas did not come under external threat during Rogers' second term, but the reappointed governor had difficulties. Still seeking to bolster the island's defenses, Rogers sought imposition of a local tax. The assembly, which had been instituted in Rogers' absence, objected, and Rogers responded by dissolving it. The governmental battle exhausted Rogers, who again went to Charleston in early 1731 in an attempt to recover his health. Though he returned in July 1731, he never truly regained his health, and died in Nassau on 15 July 1732. A harbor side street in Nassau is named for Rogers.

"Piracy expelled, commerce restored" remained the motto of the Bahamas until the islands gained independence in 1973.

Pirates pursue merchant ship

The "Flying Gang" Pirates

Jolly Roger flown by Black Sam Bellamy

How the "Flying Gang" Began

The rise of the pirate gangs who infested the Bahamas before their expulsion in 1718 was inextricably linked to the commissioning of privateers by the Jamaican government in the years following the War of the Spanish Succession.

The governor of Jamaica, Lord Archibald Hamilton commissioned Henry Jennings, Leigh Ashworth and Francis Fernandez, to protect Jamaican trade from the harassment of the Spanish Coastguard and pirates.

When these privateers shed their allegiance to the crown and turned pirate, Governor Hamilton was forced to explain his motives in commissioning them. His defense; *"having been frequently importuned by the clamors of our trading people, I was prevailed upon at last to grant commission to some to arm and cruise upon Spanish pirates."*

Corrupt Governor

Governor Hamilton's motives were not entirely altruistic, however, and as demands for reparations for the losses suffered to the pirates came in from colonial French and Spanish authorities it became clear that Hamilton himself had a financial interest in the pirate's activities.

The Spanish, who had suffered greatly at the hands of Henry Jennings and his consorts, believed that Hamilton was "part owner of all the vessels" and "owned a fourth part" of one of them.

Spain
Charles II, 1683
Silver 2 reales

Silver Coinage of the era

Governor Hamilton was also known to have received over 468 pounds of silver as his share of the profits from just one pirating voyage and was also a partner with a group building a fleet of armed fighting vessels.

Governor's Protection Wanes

As Governor Hamilton's power in Jamaica weakened and prior to his dismissal from office in May 1716, several of his "privateers", who had made illegal attacks on Spanish subjects, found it expedient to leave Jamaica and make for the island of New Providence. There they joined up with other pirates under the leadership of Benjamin Hornigold

By the end of 1716 the pirates' ranks had swollen to such an extent that they were in complete control of New Providence, Captain Jennings was appointed "their commodore" and they called themselves the "Flying Gang." Why this name was chosen is unclear.

The Flying Gang included some of the most notorious and most successful pirates of the day; as well as Jennings and Hornigold, it also included Samuel Bellamy, Edward England, Samuel Moody, Edward Teach (Black-beard) and Charles Vane.

Majority of Golden Age Pirates were "Flying Gang" members

As the crews of the Flying Gang widened their hunting grounds and captured more ships, they expanded, and then divided, creating new crews with new captains. Even after the pirates were expelled from the Bahamas in 1718 the majority of the pirate crews active in the Atlantic up to about 1722 had originated in the Flying Gang.

Some have calculated that about ninety percent of the Atlantic pirates operating between 1716 and 1726 began with the Flying Gang including the pirates George Lowther and Edward Low and ending with the execution of William Fly in 1726.

Edward Teach (Blackbeard) had sailed with Hornigold and may previously have served with Jamaican privateers. After rising to his own command he sailed in consort with Stede Bonnet, and many of the men captured with Bonnet in 1718 had joined him from Teach's crew.

Edward England may also have served in Jamaican privateers before joining the New Providence pirates. He captured a ship whose crew included Howell Davis, who in turn became a pirate after running away from New Providence

Davis also sailed alongside Thomas Cocklyn and Oliver La Bouche, both of whom had been members of the Flying Gang, and La Bouche would soon to sail with John Taylor, Edward England's successor, who had also sailed under Davis.

Paul Williams sailed with Hornigold and Samuel Bellamy and later served in La Bouche's crew.

Thomas Anstis rose to command after deserting Bartholomew Roberts, and one of his crew, John Phillips, later had command of his own ship, assisted by a quartermaster who had formerly sailed under Edward Teach, until his death in 1724.

Governments Alarmed by Flying Gang Strength

In this way it can be seen that the influence of the Flying Gang

Pirates attacking ship

was felt on pirate vessels throughout the period. The rapidly expanding strength of the Flying Gang alarmed the governments of neighboring colonies, as well as merchants whose vessels traded in the West Indies who clamored for the government in Whitehall to provide some means to end the menace.

New Governor and Military Force Sent to Quell Pirates

In September 1717 the government responded by sending an increased naval force to the area and issuing a Royal proclamation offering a free pardon to any pirates who surrendered before September 1718 and rewards for those who helped capture pirates who did not.

Former privateer and circumnavigator Woodes Rogers was appointed the new governor of the Bahamas with instructions to suppress pirates who did not take the pardon.

New Governor Arrives

When news of the proclamation reached New Providence it created a schism in the pirate community. Some men, like Henry Jennings, who had already tired of piracy, embraced the offer of pardon and sailed for Bermuda to accept it; others "rejected [it] with contempt" and proposed fortifying the island.

When Captain Vincent Pearse of HMS *Phoenix* arrived at New Providence in February 1718, 209 pirates, including several ringleaders such as Black Bart, Hornigold, Williams and Vane, surrendered to him. Less than half the pirate population at New Providence accepted the pardon, and twenty-five of those who did had returned to their old trade before Pearse and the HMS *Phoenix* left New Providence, including Vane. Still more waited until Pearse left before resuming their piracy.

Those pirates remaining at New Providence who had rejected or broken the pardon were left leaderless by the surrender of

Jennings and Hornigold, and now fell loosely under the leadership of Charles Vane.

The new Governor, Woodes Rogers arrived in the Bahamas to take up his post, supported by a company of soldiers and a strong naval force. Most of the pirates had already left by that time; only Charles Vane and his crew and a few others remained to deliver a parting shot before heading out to sea.

The Flying Gang Pirates of New Providence

This gang of pirates is responsible for virtually all of our pirate imagery today. They were also the primary inspiration for pirates of fiction from Long John Silver to Jack Sparrow.

The pirates who called themselves the Flying Gang -- all knew one another, had served together in naval and merchant vessels, and operated for a very short period of time: only several years starting in 1714.

The membership included many of the most famous pirates in history :

Blackbeard	Sam Bellamy	Edward England
Charles Vane,	Stede Bonnet,	Samuel Moody
Robert Sample	Calico Jack Rackham	George Lowther
Mary Read	Anne Bonny	Edward Low
Howell Davis	Thomas Cocklyn	Oliver La Bouche
John Taylor	William Fly	Thomas Arstis
Christopher Moody	Paulsgrave Williams	David Herriott
Thomas Cocklyn	Walter Kennedy	John Rose Archer
Captain Lane	Henry Jennings	Benjamin Hornigold

As the crews of the Flying Gang widened their hunting grounds, so they expanded and then divided, creating new crews with new captains.

The Flying Gang pirates were among history's most successful. By their peak in 1718, the Royal Navy was afraid to encounter them at all. Several of the pirates were using ships as powerful as any warship the Navy had posted in the Americas, and the pirates had two or three time the manpower.

A major reason the Flying Gang became so successful was because the "Pirate Republic" of New Providence provided them a safe haven from which they could not be easily dislodged and operate with impunity.

Notably Not on the List

One of the most famous pirates of all, Captain Kidd, began his career at the dawn of the Golden Age of Piracy" as a Privateer charged with the elimination or at least reducing piratical activities in the New World. He is not on our list and you will soon find out why

Flying Gang pirates had several motivations.

Most of them were ex-sailors revolting against tyrannical conditions on merchant and naval ships; for this reason pirates ran their ships democratically, sharing plunder equally, and selecting and deposing their captains by popular vote. Africans could be equal members of their crews – several became pirate captains – and slaves throughout the Caribbean sought to join the pirates' roughshod republic in the Bahamas.

Some Englishmen went pirate as a way of supporting a global conspiracy to restore the recently-deposed Stuart line to the British throne.

The "Flying Gang" Connections

The "Flying Gang" pirates all knew one another before establishing their "Gang.". They had served together in naval and merchant vessels and as crew together on pirate ships. Members include many of the pirates that visited New England and Cape Cod waters.

What a Wicked Web we Weave

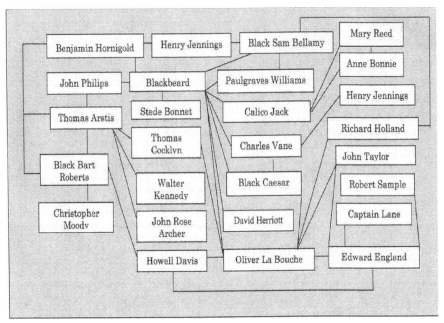

This chart illustrates the connections between the "Flying Gang" pirates that visited Cape Cod and New England waters during the "Golden Age of Piracy"

Perhaps the most famous pirate of the Golden Age was Captain William Kidd. You may have noticed his absence in the chart above. His absence is for at least two good reasons primary of which is that his career had ended with his hanging in 1701 which was well before the "Flying Gang" was established. The second reason, which will be revealed later, will probably surprise you.

Both the Flying Gang pirate fleet and the number of pirates expanded rapidly for as they captured ships new crews with new captains had to be established. More pirate ships also necessitated the widening of their hunting grounds. This expansion in the number of pirate vessels seeking plunder, combined with the end of the Spanish Gold Fleet era, required that the pirates expand their areas of activity.

The Cape Cod and New England Connection

The Gulf Stream and prevailing Trade Winds brought shipping between the Americas and Europe up along the American coast into New England waters and close to Cape Cod and the Maine coast.

It was the ever increasing number of pirate ships and the end of the Spanish gold galleon era and the Gulf Stream that brought many pirates to the northern waters of New England and to Cape Cod seeking opportunities to plunder.

Early chart showing the Gulf Stream

Forbes List of the Top-Earning Pirates

Forbes lists the highest-earning pirate ever as Samuel "Black Sam" Bellamy, an Englishman who made his bones patrolling the New England coast in the 18th century. "Black Sam" plundered an estimated $120 million over the course of his career. His greatest windfall occurred in February of 1717, when he captured the slave ship *Whydah*, which reportedly held more than four and a half tons of gold and silver. Bellamy, known for his relative generosity, took the *Whydah* as his new flagship and gave one of his old vessels to the defeated crew.

In second place, with lifetime earnings of $115 million: Sir Francis Drake, a 16th century British privateer who saved England from the Spanish Armada and went on to a profitable life of plunder at the behest of Her Majesty's Government.

Fellow Englishman Thomas Tew places third with earnings of $102 million. His biggest score came in 1693, when he pilfered a ship full of gold en route to the Ottoman Empire from India.

Wealth estimates are based on information gathered from historical records and accounts from 17th and 18th century sources like Daniel Defoe, as well as contemporary historians like David Cordingly. Whenever possible, official records of pirate's claims were used. So when a 1718 North Carolina ledger reports wares seized from Edward "Blackbeard" Teach sold at market for 2,500 pounds following his death. That source was trusted above Blackbeard's claims to a magistrate that a great treasure lay in a location known only to him and the devil. By our count, he amassed a total of $12.5 million in loot over his career.

Depletion of fortune due to rum and wenches was not assessed, nor were divisions of treasure among the crew. All money and goods were converted into present value U.S. dollars. Present values were determined using the retail price index developed by the British House of Commons and Measuring Worth, a research project founded by University of Illinois Chicago economics professor Lawrence H. Officer.

Pirates didn't have 401(k) plans, so burying a pile of gold was sometimes the smartest way to save for the future–that is, when they had one. Samuel Bellamy's treasure sank with him off Cape Cod, most of Bartholomew Roberts' fortune ($32 million) was taken after he died in battle in 1722 and Stede Bonnet's wealth ($4.4 million) was absorbed into the South Carolina treasury after his 1718 execution. Jean Fleury's Aztec gold wasn't recovered and was probably spread thin over brothels and saloons from Cuba to France; it's likely been melted down over the last 500 years into gold bars lining national treasuries and formed into wedding rings the world over.

Most pirates died without honor or coin. It was an existence filled with murder, treachery, disease (both tropical and venereal), and it ensured a short life, even by the standards of the day. But for the chance to be rich and unbound from a life of farming or military service, it was an easy choice for many– even if it did come with scurvy.

From an article by Matt Woolsey 9/19/2008 on www.forbes.com

This Top Earning Pirates listing, although interesting, is not entirely correct as we shall soon see.

Forbes List of the Top-Earning Pirates

The 20 Highest-Earning Pirates

Pirate	Wealth (2013 dollars)
Samuel "Black Sam" Bellamy	$130.2 million
Sir Francis Drake	$124.7 million
Thomas Tew	$111.7 million
John Bowen	$43.4 million
Bartholomew "Black Bart" Roberts	$34.7 million
Jean Fleury	$34.2 million
Thomas White	$16 million
John Halsey	$14.1 million
Harry Morgan	$14.1 million
Edward "Blackbeard" Teach	$13.6 million
Samuel Burgess	$10.3 million
Edward England	$8.7 million
Francois le Clerc	$8.1 million
Howell Davis	$4.9 million
Stede Bonnet	$4.9 million
Richard Worley	$3.8 million
Charles Vane	$2.5 million
Edward Low	$2 million
John Rackam	$1.6 million
James Martel	$1.6 million

Bold denotes "Flying Gang" member

Excerpted from Forbes article by Matt Woolsey 9/19/2008

The Most Famous Pirate?

Capt. William Kidd
Was he the Bad Luck Kidd?

Kidd was born in 1645 into a respectable family at Greenock, Scotland. He had settled in New York and was a successful sea captain. In 1695, at the age of 49, the governor of New York and Massachusetts, Richard Coote, enlisted Kidd's aide in reducing the piratical activities of such infamous pirates as Thomas Tew, John Ireland and Thomas Wake as well as any enemy French shipping. Thus William Kidd's career began as a privateer and not as a pirate. In fact, we shall see that perhaps Captain Kidd was never a pirate at all!

Captain William Kidd

Purchased Rather than Plundered

Kidd purchased a new vessel, hardly something a real pirate would do, that he named *Adventurer*. It was a galley of 284 tons which he equipped with thirty four cannon. He then recruited a sizeable crew of only the finest sailors of the day.

Bad luck found Kidd almost immediately – while in mid-ocean the British navy stopped his vessel and "recruited" most of Kidd's handpicked mariners thereby forcing him back to shore to replenish his now depleted crew.

Unfortunately, because the Royal Navy had immediately preceded him, the only sailors left represented a miserable mix of former pirates and hardened criminals. Bad luck again, but Kidd forged ahead confident in his abilities to accomplish his goals.

Crew Decimated by Disease

He set to sea once more only to have a sudden and ghastly attack of cholera decimate and kill more than a third of his crew. This bit of bad luck caused Kidd to remain at anchor while he again went ashore to find replacements for his dead crewmembers. This last bit of luck, however, had a positive aspect. While at anchor Kidd discovered fatal flaws in his new ship's construction, flaws that certainly would have caused the *Adventurer* to sink in the first storm it encountered while at sea.

Intent upon completing his mission, Kidd stole a French ship and immediately began his quest to capture pirates and French shipping. More bad luck – Try as they might, not a pirate or French ship could they find. Therefore, by the end of 1697, the crew was becoming restless and mutiny was in the air. Kidd finally agreed to attack any non-English vessel, not just French or pirate ships.

More Bad Luck

Captain Kidd returned to New York after a year of successful privateering only to find he had been betrayed by his backers and the governor. He was now a wanted man and charged with piracy.

Kidd, using his lawyer as intermediary, negotiated with the governor in Boston for safe entry into the city. Bad luck and deceit – again he was betrayed, this time by his own lawyer, (surprise of surprises) and he and his motley crew were thrust into Stone Prison to await trial as pirates.

More than a year later, most of which time Kidd spent in solitary confinement, Captain Kidd was sent to England to be tried for piracy upon the high seas and murder. His pleas for clemency in letters to King William III, allegedly one of the backers, were ignored. On May 23rd, 1701, he was hanged at Execution Dock in London.

Even his Letter of Marque had his name wrong!

This Letter of Marque was granted to one Captain <u>Robert</u> Kidd who is believed to actually be Captain William Kidd as it was issued contemporaneously and with the same charge issued by Governor Richard Coote.

William Rex,

William the Third, by the grace of God, King of England, Scotland, France and Ireland, defender of the faith, &c. To our trusty and well beloved Capt. Robert Kidd, commander of the same for the time being,

Greeting: whereas we are informed, that Capt. Thomas Too, John Ireland, Capt. Thomas Wake, and Capt. William Maze or Mace, and other subjects, natives or inhabitants of New-York, and elsewhere, in our plantations in America, have associated themselves with divers others, wicked and ill-disposed persons, and do, against the law of nations, commit many and great piracies, robberies and depredations on the seas upon the parts of America, and in other parts, to the great hindrance and discouragement of trade and navigation, and to the great danger and hurt of our loving subjects, our allies, and all others, navigating the seas upon their lawful occasions.

Now know ye, that we being desirous to prevent the aforesaid mischiefs, and as much as in us lies, to bring the said pirates, free-booters and sea-rovers to justice, have thought fit, and do hereby give and grant to the said Robert Kidd, (to whom our commissioners for exercising the office of Lord High Admiral of England, have granted a commission as a private man-of-war, bearing date the 11th day of December, 1695,) and unto the commander of the said ship for the time being, and unto the officers, mariners, and others which shall be under your command, full power and authority to apprehend, seize, and take into your custody as well the said Capt. Thomas Too, John Ireland, Capt. Thomas Wake and Capt. Wm. Maze or Mace, as all such pirates, free-booters, and sea-rovers, being either our subjects, or of other nations associated with them, which you shall meet with upon the seas or coasts, with all their ships and vessels, and all such merchandizes, money, goods, and wares as shall be found on board, or with them, in case they shall willingly yield themselves; but if they will not yield without fighting, then you are by force to compel them to yield.

And we also require you to bring, or cause to be brought, such pirates, free-booters, or sea-rovers, as you shall seize, to a legal trial, to the end they may be proceeded against according to the law in such cases. And we do hereby command all our officers, ministers, and other our loving subjects whatsoever, to be aiding and assisting to you in the premises.

And we do hereby enjoin you to keep an exact journal of your proceedings in execution of the premises, and set down the names of such pirates, and of their officers and company, and the names of such ships and vessels as you shall by virtue of these presents take and seize, and the quantities of arms, ammunition, provision, and lading of such ships, and the true value of the same, as near as you can judge.

And we do hereby strictly charge and command you, as you will answer the contrary at your peril, that you do not, in any manner, offend or molest our friends or allies, their ships or subjects, by colour or pretence of these presents, or the authority thereby granted.

In witness whereof, we have caused our great seal of England to be affixed to these presents.

Given at our court in Kensington, the 26th day of January, 1695, in the 7th year of our reign.

Kidd's Admission of Buried Treasure Ignored

After receiving the death penalty, Captain Kidd wrote the following letter to Robert Harley, Speaker of the House of Commons from Newgate Prison offering to lead the government's representative to treasure he had buried in the "Indies." However, the Speaker ignored the letter considering it a desperate attempt to save his neck from the gallows and the letter of the law.

S'r,

The sence of my present Condition (being under Condemnation) and the thoughts of having bene imposed on by such as seek't my destruction thereby to fulfill their ambitious desires makes me uncapable of Expressing my selfe in those terms as I ought, therefore due most humbly pray that you will be pleased to represent to the Hon'bl. house of Comons that in my late proceedings in the Indies I have lodged goods and Tresure to the value of one hundred thousand pounds, which I desire the Government may have the benefitt of, in order thereto, I shall desire no manner of liberty but to be kept prisoner on board such shipp as may be appointed for that purpose, and only give the necessary directions and in case I faile therin I desire no favour but to be forthwith Executed according to my Sentence. If y'r honbl. house will please to order a Comittee to come to me, I doubt not but to give such satisfaction as may obtaine mercy, most Humbly submitting to the wisdom of your great assembly I am

S'r Y'r Unfortunate humble servant

(The actual signature of Wm Kidd on the last letter he would ever write)

Capt Kidd Treasure Maps

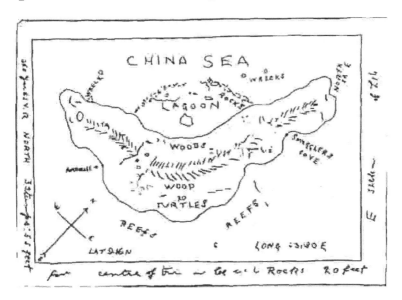

Found in what is believed to be Captain Kidd's sea chest
in England

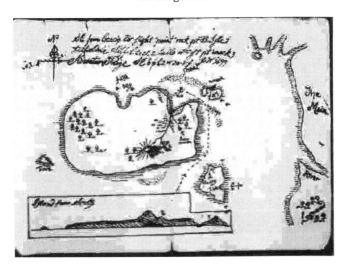

Kidd's Treasure Map found in
New England by the late Edward Rowe Snow

Captain Kidd's Buried Treasure

There is more buried treasure attributed to Captain Kidd than to any other pirate. Kidd's treasure is reported to be buried at: Block, Patience, Hope, Conanicut and Hog islands in Rhodes Island, Charles and the Thimble islands in Connecticut, Gardiner and Long islands and various islands in the Hudson in New York, Plum Island and Cape Cod in Massachusetts, Isles of Shoals off Maine and New Hampshire, various islands in Penobscot Bay and elsewhere along the Maine coast and Oak Island in Nova Scotia.

There are several accounts that have Kidd burying his loot as he made his way from the Caribbean to New York and Boston. Some say he buried his loot in order to avoid splitting all of it with his backers. Others believe he had caught wind of being accused of piracy and was hiding the treasure to use as a bargaining chip in case he was captured.

More Treasure Secreted In the Indies

The governor wrote in July of 1699. . .

"Captain Kidd in a sloop richly laden, came to Rhode Island, and sent one Emmot to Boston to treat about his admission and security. He said Kidd had left the great Moorish ship he took in India, called the Quedagh Merchant, in a creek on the coast of Hispaniola, with goods to the value of £30,000.

New Law Just for Kidd

In 1700 a new law was introduced to allow for the swift trial and execution of pirates wherever they may be found. Previously they had to be transported back to London to stand trial and be executed at the low tide mark at Wapping. The *'Act for the More Effectual Suppression of Piracy'* also enforced the use of the death penalty and gave rewards for resisting pirate attack, but most importantly, it was *not trial by jury* but by a special court of naval officers.

Captain Kidd was one of the first victims of this new law - indeed the law was partially rushed through specifically <u>so that it could be applied to him.</u> Reasoning being he would be more likely to be convicted by the naval officer's he was charged with attacking than he would by a jury of civilians.

Bad Luck Streak Continues

Captain Kidd's body gibbeted in London

More bad luck even while on the gallows. The trap door was sprung and Captain William Kidd fell to meet his maker but ... the hangman's rope broke! He had to be hung a second time, and this time the rope held.

However, just before his six associates that were convicted along with him were to be hanged, a messenger arrived with a pardon from the king and they were set free. They were spared but Captain Kidd, even with the extra time the broken rope gave him, went to his death with his bad luck streak unbroken.

The authorities painted Kidd's body with tar, wrapped it in chains, placed it in an iron cage, and hung him overlooking the Thames River, London. For nearly two years his body remained gibbeted as an example to deter other would-be-pirates.

More Bad Luck Even After his Death

Nearly three hundred years after his hanging, documents that had been misfiled at the time of his trial were uncovered and, if available then, would have exonerated him of all charges of wrong doing. Three hundred years after his death, Captain William Kidd is proven to have been innocent of all charges.

Captain Kidd was not a pirate

Pirate Hornigold's

Vocational Training Ship Graduates

Blackbeard

Black Caesar

Black Sam Bellamy

Black Bart Roberts

Paulgraves Williams

Henry Jennings

John Phillips

Oliver La Buse

PIRATE CERTIFICATE

The kingdom hereby certifies that the undersigned is now an official pirate

Benjamin Hornigold

Little is known of Benjamin Hornigold until 1713 and the signing of The Treaty of Utrecht that ended the War of the Spanish Succession (also known as Queen Anne's War). The Treaty ended hostilities between Spain, France, the Netherlands, and Britain.

With the cessation of the war, all English letters of marque granted to privateers became null and void. This put many privateers out of work and some "went on the account" (became pirates). Benjamin Hornigold may have been one of these men, but he still considered himself a true privateer and, as such, attacked only shipping of enemies of the English.

His first act of Piracy was in August of 1713, only months after the end of the War of Spanish Succession, when he employed small sailing canoes and a sloop to attack merchant vessels off the coast of New Providence.

Pirates attacking larger ship

Established the Pirate's Republic

He took residence at Nassau, which had been almost completely destroyed during the war. It was here that Hornigold and his colleague and fellow pirate, John Cockram, built the foundations of the famous pirate society in the Bahamas also known as the Pirate's Republic of New Providence.

John Cockram had moved to Harbour Island some 50 miles from Nassau, where he married the daughter of a Leading merchant. After settling there he quickly established an

74

advanced smuggling, supply, and money-laundering operation for Hornigold and his growing cohort of pirates.

In 1715 many adventurers, treasure seekers and would be pirates, including Sam Bellamy and Palgrave's Williams, came into Nassau because of the wreck of a Spanish treasure fleet on the nearby coast of Florida.

Hornigold's Pirate Vocational Training Ship

The pirate population at Hornigold's Pirate Republic at New Providence grew exponentially. By early 1716 Hornigold's own pirate crew had grown to over 200 men!

In April 1716 Hornigold gave shelter to two novice pirates who had just stolen a large amount of treasure from Jennings' Gang. These men, after Hornigold's training, where to become successful pirates captains themselves in the near future; Samuel Bellamy and Paulgrave Williams. Edward Teach a/k/a Blackbeard and scores of others also would begin their pirating careers as a Hornigold trainee.

Sometime after Bellamy and Williams joined Hornigold's crew. Hornigold teamed up with a French Pirate who would become one of the most successful pirates of the Golden Age of Piracy, Olivier La Buse.

Together they raided Spanish vessels through the summer of 1716. By 1717 Hornigold had gained command of a 30 gun sloop named the *Ranger* which was likely the most heavily armed vessel in the Bahamas and let him overpower any ship with ease. The captain of this vessel later reported that Hornigold's fleet now had **5** Vessels and a combined Crew of around 350 Pirates!

Ship similar to Hornigold's **Ranger**

In May 1716 the *Boston News Letter* reported that after capturing a French ship, Hornigold informed the master that *"they never consented to the Articles of Peace with the French and Spaniards"* and that *"they meddle not with the English or Dutch."*

After reading this account, Alexander Spotswood, Governor of Virginia and an ardent enemy of pirates, thought otherwise. In a letter to his superiors, he wrote:

> *. . .there is so little trust to be given to such a People, that it is not to be doubted they will use all Nations alike whenever they have an advantage.*

New Providence an "Impending Danger"

Hornigold's base of operations in New Providence was located near the Straits of Florida, the main shipping lane that vessels bound for Latin America, America's coast or back to Europe traveled and therefore a perfect place for a pirate haven.

The numerous islands, cays, and islets that comprise the Bahamas provided myriad hidden shelters for pirate vessels and plenty of food and fresh water to feed their crews.

Governor Spotswood was aware of this new "nest of pirates" and impending danger it presented. In July 1716, he forwarded to the Council of Trade and Plantations in London the deposition of John Vickers, who had recently come from New Providence.

Nest of pirates

In Nov. last Benjamin Hornigold arrived at Providence in the sloop Mary *of Jamaica, belonging to Augustine Golding, which Hornigold took upon the Spanish coast, and soon after the taking of the said sloop, he took a Spanish sloop loaded with dry goods and sugar, which cargo he disposed of at Providence, but the Spanish sloop was taken from him by Capt. Jennings of the sloop Bathsheba of Jamaica. In January Hornigold sailed from Providence in the said sloop* Mary, *having on board 140 men, 6 guns and 8 swivel guns, and soon after returned with another Spanish sloop, which he took on the coast of Florida. After he had fitted the said sloop at Providence, he sent Golding's sloop back to Jamaica to be returned to the owners: and in March last sailed from Providence in the said Spanish sloop, having on board near 200 men, but whither bound deponent knoweth not.*

These pirates weren't the only riffraff plaguing the islands, for Vickers also described around fifty others who had plundered the wrecks of treasure galleons.

[They] committ great disorders in that Island, plundering the inhabitants, burning their houses, and ravishing their wives. One Thomas Barrow formerly mate of a Jamaica brigantine which run away some time ago with a Spanish marquiss's money and effects, is the chief of them and gives out that he only waits for a vessell to go out a pirating, that he is Governor of Providence and will make it a second Madagascar, and expects 5 or 600 men more from Jamaica sloops to join in the settling of Providence, and to make war on the French and Spaniards, but for the English, they don't intend to meddle with them, unless they are first attack'd by them . . . .

The Lord Proprietors had basically abandoned the Bahamas in 1703, which made it easier for the pirates to gain control. Thomas Walker acted as the deputy governor, but even he was powerless against these men as shown in Vickers' deposition, which can be found in the *Calendar of State Papers Colonial, America and West Indies.*

About a year ago one Daniel Stillwell formerly belonging to Jamaica, and lately settled on Isle Aethera, went in a small shallop, with John Kemp, Matthew Low, two Dutchmen, and – Darvell to the coast of Cuba and there took a Spanish lanch [launch] having on board 11,050 pieces of eight, and brought the same into Isle Aethera; and Capt. Thomas Walker of Providence having received advice thereof from the Governor of Jamaica, seized Stillwell and his vessell, but upon the coming of Hornigold to Providence, Stillwell was rescued and Capt. Walker threatned to have his house burned for offering to concern himself, Hornigold saying that all pirates were under his protection. . . . Signed, John Vickers.

The "Flying Gang" is established

Hornigold and his cohorts adopted the moniker "the Flying Gang." Vickers wasn't the only one to provide eyewitness testimony to what had befallen New Providence and the risk the pirates' presence posed to good English citizens because of the raids on Spanish vessels and territories.

Captain Walker wrote:

I was formerly directed by H.E. Genll. Nicholson to render to your Lordships an accot. of the state and condition of ye Bohamia Islands wch. has a long time bin without governmts., The want of wch. has laid those Islands open to be a recepticall and shelter of pirates and loose fellows and gives ye inhabitants as well as ye trading vessuals from other parts ye liberty and oppertunity of inriching themselves by sideing and dealing with, entertaining and releiveing such villians who from time to time resort there to sell and dispose of their piraticall goods, and perfusely spend wtt.[what?] they take from ye English, French and mostly Spaniards, and as I am an inhabitant of New Providence have bin an eye witness to those ellegiall and unwarrantable practises commited both by ye piratts and inhabitants and others tradeing there, and have used ye uttmost of my endeavours to put by and prevent them, as alsoe by my goeing to the Havana hath bin a means of preventing ye design of ye provoked Spaniards comeing to cut those Islands off for the piraces ytt. has since ye peace bin commited even by some of the inhabitants of those Islands

The pirates daly increse to Providence and haveing began to mount ye guns in ye Fort for there[their] defence and seeking ye oppertunity to kill mee because I was against their illegall and unwarrantable practices and by no means would consent to their mounting of guns in ye Fort upon such accots. I was thereupon forced with my wife and family to acquitt ye Island to my great expence and damage and ye latter part of June last arrived safe to this Province [South Carolina] where I remaine upon expence in hopes thatt H.M.[His Majesty] will be gratiously pleased to take those Islands under his care and

78

protection, etc. that ye Islands may become a flourishing plantation, etc.

In 1717 Captain Matthew Munthe went pirate hunting on orders from Deputy Governor Robert Daniel of South Carolina, who was concerned about the effects such men would have on trade and the citizenry of the colony. An accident prevented Munthe from carrying out part of his orders, but he did send Daniel a report that included:

Gold and silver pieces of eight

Five pirates made ye harbor of Providence their place of rendezvous vizt. Horngold, a sloop with 10 guns and about 80 men; Jennings, a sloop with 10 guns and 100 men; Burgiss, a sloop with 8 guns and about 80 men; White, in a small vessel with 30 men and small arms; Thatch, a sloop 6 gunns and about 70 men.

Hornigold's many ships

During his time as a pirate, Hornigold used a variety of vessels. His first sloop was *Happy Return*, although he merely sailed her. Jonathan Darvell owned the sloop; unhappy with his share of the profits, Hornigold and two other men bought a boat from an Eleutheran. With this they captured two Cuban vessels carrying treasure valued at 46,000 pieces of eight.

In 1715 he seized a sloop-of-war, which he christened *Benjamin*. Two hundred pirates manned her. When he later parted company with Samuel Bellamy, he sailed a smaller sloop named *Adventure*. He captured and then captained a sloop named *Ranger* armed with thirty guns.

At this point Benjamin Hornigold was one of the four most influential pirates at New Providence. The others were Henry Jennings, Josiah Burgess, and Edward "Blackbeard" Teach. The last had learned the tricks of his trade from Hornigold, who recognized Teach's talents early on and mentored him. As for Jennings, he considered Hornigold his rival. For example, in 1716 Jennings tried to steal a rich prize Hornigold had captured, but that crafty pirate eluded him.

Not long after Hornigold escaped Jennings' clutches, Samuel Bellamy, Paulsgrave Williams, and their men asked to join up with Hornigold. These audacious men, recently from New England, had just stolen treasure from Jennings. This impressed Hornigold, who not only welcomed them, but made Bellamy captain of the *Marianne*, even though others from his own crew, including Edward Teach, were more deserving.

When Olivier La Buse, captain of the *Postillion*, and his men happened upon this new fleet of pirates, they decided to sail in consort. Together they sailed the West Indies in search of prey, capturing forty-one prizes in less than one year.

Dissention re: attacks on British culminates

When an English sail was sighted, the pirates wanted to attack. Hornigold did not, but since majority ruled amongst the brethren, they attacked the vessel. Amongst those captured was twenty-five-year-old John Brown, who gave testimony about what happened on 6 May 1717.

> *About a year agoe he belonged to a Ship commanded by Captain Kingston, which in her voyage with Logwood to Holland was taken to the Leeward of the Havana by two Piratical Sloops, one commanded by Hornygold and the other by a Frenchman called Leboose, each having 70 men on board.*

> *The pirats kept the Ship about 8 or 10 daies, and then having taken out off her what they thought proper delivered her back to some of the men, who belonged to her. Leboose kept the Examinate on board his Sloop about 4 months, the English Sloop under Hornigolds command keeping company with them all that time.*

Off Cape Corante they took two Spanish Briganteens without any resistance, laden with cocoa from Ma[l]aca. The Spaniards, not coming up to the pirats demand about the ransom, were put ashoar and their Briganteens burn'd.

They sailled next to the Isle of Pines, where meeting with three or four English Sloops empty, they made use of them in cleaning their own, and gave them back. From thence they sailled in the latter end of May to Hispaniola, where they tarried about 3 months.

The Examinate then left Leboose and went on board the Sloop commanded formerly by Hornygold, but at that time by one Bellamy, who upon a difference arising amongst the English Pirats because Hornygold refused to take and plunder English Vessels, was chosen by a great majority their Captain, and Hornygold departed with 26 hands in a Prize Sloop . . . .

Among those loyal followers was Edward Teach, but within a few months, he, too, followed his own path to become one of the most feared pirates of the era, *Blackbeard*.

Controversy as to who replaced Hornigold

Most say Hornigold was overthrown by Edward Teach one such source that claims this is the book *Konstam, Blackbeard: America's Most Notorious Pirate.*

It states that in November 1717 a vote was taken among the combined crews to attack any vessel they chose. Hornigold opposed the decision and was voted out of his rank as captain and replaced by Edward Teach.

Another source claims that it was Samuel Bellamy who was the replacement captain after Hornigold was voted out.

It states that around June of 1716, Bellamy challenged Hornigold for the position of captain, as he was growing more and more irritated by Hornigold's refusal to attack ships of England. a vote was to be taken in which the crew decided who would become captain. Hornigold lost the election and was deposed as captain.

King's offer to Pardon pirates

By now the British Crown could no longer ignore the pleas of merchants and citizens to suppress the pirates. To that end George II issued this royal proclamation on 5 September 1717:

Whereas We have received Information, That several Persons, Subjects of Great Britain, have, since the Twenty fourth Day of June, in the Year of our Lord One thousand seven hundred and fifteen, committed divers Piracies and Robberies upon the High Seas in the West-Indies, or adjoyning to Our Plantations, which hath, and may Occasion great Damage to the

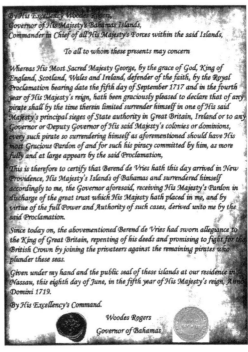

By His Excellency Woodes Rogers,
Governor of His Majesty's Bahama Islands,
Commander in Chief of all His Majesty's Forces within the said Islands,

To all to whom these presents may concern

Whereas His Most Sacred Majesty George, by the grace of God, King of England, Scotland, Wales and Ireland, defender of the faith, by the Royal Proclamation bearing date the fifth day of September 1717 and in the fourth year of His Majesty's reign, hath been graciously pleased to declare that of any pirate shall by the time therein limited surrender himself in one of His said Majesty's principal sieges of State authority in Great Britain, Ireland or to any Governor or Deputy Governor of His said Majesty's colonies or dominions, every such pirate so surrendering himself as aforementioned should have His most Gracious Pardon of and for such his piracy committed by him, as more fully and at large appears by the said Proclamation.

This is therefore to certify that Berend de Vries hath this day arrived in New Providence, His Majesty's Islands of Bahamas and surrendered himself accordingly to me, the Governor aforesaid, receiving His Majesty's Pardon in discharge of the great trust which His Majesty hath placed in me, and by virtue of the full Power and Authority of such cases, derived unto me by the said Proclamation.

Since today on, the abovementioned Berend de Vries had sworn allegiance to the King of Great Britain, repenting of his deeds and promising to fight for the British Crown by joining the privateers against the remaining pirates who plunder these seas.

Given under my hand and the public seal of these islands at our residence in Nassau, this eighth day of June, in the fifth year of His Majesty's reign, Anno Domini 1719.

By His Excellency's Command.

Woodes Rogers
Governor of Bahamas

King's Pardon

Merchants of Great Britain, and others, Trading into those Parts; And though We have appointed such a Force as We Judge sufficient for Suppressing the said Piracies: Yet the more effectually to put an End to the same, We have thought fit, by and with the Advice of our Privy-Council, to Issue this Our Royal Proclamation; And We do hereby Promise and Declare, That in case any of the said Pirates shall, on or before the Fifth Day of September, in the Year of our Lord One thousand seven hundred and eighteen, Surrender him or themselves to One of Our Principal Secretaries of State in Great Britain or Ireland, or to any Governor or Deputy-Governor of any of Our Plantations or Dominions beyond the Seas, every such Pirate and Pirates, so Surrendring him or themselves, as

aforesaid, shall have Our Gracious Pardon of and for
such his or their Piracy or Piracies, by him or them.

News of this amnesty reached the Bahamas in December. The following February HMS *Phoenix*, a small frigate in the Royal Navy, arrived in Nassau. Captain Vincent Pearse noted fourteen other ships in the harbor. These flew the colors of the Netherlands, England, France, Spain, or the flags of no nation – the Jolly Roger.

Five were indeed prizes, but nine belonged to traders who did business with the pirates, although they "pretended they never did it until after the Act of Grace was published," according to Pearse. He sent Lieutenant Symonds ashore under a flag of truce to deliver the royal proclamation. "He was received by a great number of Pirates with much Civility."

Those who were for taking the pardon provided information to the lieutenant as to where to find Charles Vane, Edward England, and their men.

On hearing the news of Vane's surrender and arrest, the pirate leaders – which included Benjamin Hornigold, Francis Lesley, Josiah Burgess, and Thomas Nichols – told Captain Pearse *"that my taking the sloop had very much alarm[ed] all, the Pyrates in general believing that men taken in her would be executed."* They counseled Pearse that releasing the pirates *"would be a very great means to induce [them] to surrender and accept the Act of Grace."*

Pearse apparently felt their advice merited consideration, for he did release Vane, England, and fourteen others. Only one pirate, named Lark, remained under arrest.

Benjamin Hornigold felt they should take the pardon. Thereafter, they could either become members of society or return to their old ways later if they wished. Most of the brethren concurred. The morning of 26 February 1718 and for the next two days, the pirates ventured out to the *Phoenix* to surrender. Hornigold was one of the first to do so. In all 209 pirates received certificates of protection.

The new Governor of the Bahamas, Woodes Rogers wrote to the Council of Trade and Plantations:

I met with little opposition in coming in, but found a French ship.(that was taken by the pirates of 22 guns) burning in the harbour, which we were told was set on fire to drive out H.M.S. the Rose who got in too eagerly the evening before me, and cut here[her] cables and run out in the night for fear of being burnt, by one Charles Vane who command'd the pirates and at ours and H.M.S. the Milford's near approach the next morning they finding it impossible to escape us, he with about 90 men fled away in a sloop wearing the black flag, and fir'd guns of defiance when they perceiv'd their sloop out sayl'd the two that I sent to chase them hence. On the 27th I landed and took possession of the fort, where I read H.M. Commission in the presence of my officers, soldiers and about 300 of the people found here, who received me under armes and readily surrendered, shewing then many tokens of joy for the re-introduction of Governmt. I sent officers ashoar at first coming in, but by means of our ship and H.M. ship the Milford running aground I delayed my landing till this day.

Vane had decided not to take the pardon after all, but Hornigold did. Before long Governor Rogers decided the best way to capture a pirate was to hire a reformed one to bring his former colleagues to justice. He selected Hornigold, and others, for the task. Hornigold directed all the talent and ferocity that had made him a successful pirate to accomplishing his new charge. His primary target was Vane. Rogers wrote:

. . . every minute [we expected] to hear of Vaine . . . for on 1st Sepr. three men that came in a boat from Vaine who was then on the coast of Cuba confess'd they promised to meet him again about this time there; And the very day after Capt. Whitney sailed, I had an express sent me that three vessels supposed to be Vaine and his prizes were at Green Turtle Key near Abacoa and since I had no strenght to do better, I got a sloop fitted under the command of Capt. Hornygold to send and view them and bring me an accot. what they were. . .

As each day passed and no word arrived from Hornigold, Rogers worried that he had made the wrong decision in trusting the former pirate, whom he feared had joined forces with Vane.

> *. . . but to my great satisfaction he return'd in about three weeks having lain most of that time concealed and viewing of Vaine the Pirate in order to surprize him or some of his men that they expected would be near them in their boats, but tho they failed in this Capt. Hornygold brought wth. him a sloop of this place, that got leave from me to go out a turtling but had been trading wth. Vaine who had then wth. him two ships and a brigantine, his sloop that he escaped hence in being run away with by another set of new pirates, the two ships he took coming out of Carolina one of 400 and the other of 200 tons loaded wth. rice, pitch and tarr and skins bound for London the* Neptune *Capt. King being the largest he sunk and the* Emperour *Capt. Arnold Gowers he left without doing her any damage except taking away their provisions. I have secured the mercht. that traded wth. Vaine and having not yet a power to make an example of them here he remains in irons to be sent home to England by the next ship.*

> *. . . Capt. Hornygold having proved honest, and disobliged his old friends by seazing this vessel it devides the people here and makes me stronger then*[than] *I expected.*

In a subsequent letter, following Hornigold's successful capture of John Auger and twelve others, Rogers wrote, "I am glad of this new proof that Capt'n Hornigold has given to the world to wipe off the infamous name he has hither been known by Though he has admitted most people spoke well of his generosity."

Pirates Attack and Steal Only Hats!

Hornigold seized a sloop off the Honduran coast and . . .

> *"They did us no further injury than the taking most of our hats from us, having got drunk the night before, as they told us, and toss'd theirs overboard."*

Hornigold detained another sloop for two weeks before allowing - *"her to proceed on her voyage having taken very little from her (to wit) only some rum, a little sugar, powder and shott, cordage and small sayles and four gun carriages with some provisions."*

When and how Benjamin Hornigold died is a mystery. Captain Johnson said he *". . . was cast away upon rocks, a great way from land, and perished. . . ."* Most likely he encountered a hurricane, somewhere in the Caribbean or Gulf of Mexico, and drowned when his ship sank, or the ship grounded and he was among those lost. When Woodes Rogers sent a letter to his superiors in London in February 1720, he complained that he needed ships to protect the colony, but said nothing of Benjamin Hornigold. Most likely because he had probably died.

There are two theories about *Hornigold's end*

One is the most believed one is that in late 1719 when Hornigold was sent to Mexico on a trading voyage Hornigold's ship was caught in a Hurricane somewhere between New Providence and Mexico, and was wrecked on an uncharted reef far away from land. It is presumed that here he perished.

According to contemporary account *A General History of the Pyrates by Captain Charles Johnson* Hornigold indeed perished in this incident but as it states "five of his men got into a canoe and were saved" The location of the reef remains a mystery to this day.

Another source (being the book *The republic of Pirates*) states that Hornigold after his days as a Pirate-Hunter, during the *war of the Quadruple Alliance,* had received a privateering commission from Woodes Rogers and again sailed out against the Spanish. It is rumored he was captured near Havana in the spring of 1719 and was never heard from again.

Black" Sam Bellamy

Shipwrecks, Witches, Treachery, Sunken Treasure and, Ghosts

Samuel Bellamy was born in Devonshire, England in 1689. In the early 1700s, as a young teen, he left England to seek his fortune in the West Indies where he joined Captain Henry Jennings (later a Flying Gang member) and the British privateer fleet then at war against Spain. He was berthed aboard the sloop *Barsheba* and based at Port Royal in Jamaica.

Wax statue of Bellamy at the Provincetown Pirate Museum

Sam Bellamy was a large black-haired man. He is reported to have been an intelligent and popular leader of men with a reputation for being generous to his victims. Some would later refer to him as the "Prince of Pirates".

It was the time spent in the Caribbean as a privateer that he heard the stories of fantastic wealth lying on the bottom of the sea just waiting to be found. Tales of the sunken Spanish treasure that would make a man richer than any king in Europe were standard seaman issue of the era. It was here that he also was exposed to some of the strategies and techniques he would later use during his short and very successful pirating career.

He made the decision to leave his wife and child in Canterbury, England and go back to the Caribbean, retrieve the legendary Spanish treasures and return a rich man.

Retrieve Treasure from Sunken Galleons

His original plan was to locate and retrieve treasurer from a fleet of Spanish galleons that were known to have sunk off the Florida coast a year earlier in 1715. The tales of this and other sunken Spanish galleon fleets that were laden with silver and gold had flamed the imagination of adventuresome young men in Europe for hundreds of years.

Perhaps the most famous of these stories was of Philip IV's treasure ship fleet heavily laden with riches that was destroyed in a great storm as it began its return to Spain.

King Philip IV depended upon the gold, silver, and copper treasures extracted from Spain's mines in the New World to fund his vast military establishment. However, the fleet of 1622 was delayed in sailing and left Havana at the height of the hurricane season.

The entire fleet was lost when it sailed into the teeth of a violent hurricane. Remnants of this fleet are being found off Florida's coast even to this day. To provide a sense of scale to the enormity of this lost treasure, more than four tons of silver and gold have been reportedly retrieved from one wreck alone!

The thoughts of vast treasure apparently provided motive enough for Sam Bellamy to leave his wife and child half a world away. The lure of treasure allowed him to be successful in persuading a wealthy patron to finance a ship and crew to enable his adventure. After fitting out his newly acquired sloop with sufficient provisions and gear, he and his crew set of for the New World early in 1716.

According to folklore he came ashore at Eastham Harbor, Cape Cod apparently to find rest and provisions before his continued trip south to Florida.

The Saga of Maria "Goody" Hallett – *Bellamy's Paramour*

It was here that young Sam Bellamy met and seduced the very beautiful Eastham farm girl, Maria Hallett, in the spring of 1716. Maria was a naïve fifteen year old farm girl from a well respected, church going Eastham family.

The handsome sailor's sweet talk and tales of treasure and adventure impressed the wide-eyed Maria. He convinced her that he would marry her when he returned laden with silver, gold and jewels that he would recover from sunken treasure ships in the Caribbean. As Fall approached and the days shortened and grew cooler, he sailed south to begin his great adventure.

Maria "Goody" Hallett

That Winter Maria was found lying in a cold Eastham barn with her dead baby in her arms. She was at once taken into town and attached to deacon Doane's whipping post and given several lashes before being thrown into jail. The selectmen spoke of charging her with murder. They said she must be made an example to others of the godless younger generation of the day.

It seemed that no cell could contain the young lass, and she continually escaped to wander the shore calling out the name of her lost love. Eastham gave up its attempts to keep her in jail and released the young girl upon the condition she would leave town and never return.

She made her home in a shack near the shore at South Wellfleet and eked out a living by doing menial jobs. In short order, the once most beautiful girl in Eastham had become haggard and worn and unrecognizable to those who had known her before Bellamy.

His Lover Labeled a Witch

Townspeople were convinced that she was a witch, and they now referred to as "Goody" Hallett. The name Goody, as defined in the American College Dictionary, was "a polite term applied to a woman in humble life."

Goody must have been extremely depressed and traumatized experiencing the death of her baby. Then to be shunned by friends and family, jailed then driven out of town combined, perhaps causing her to lose her mind.

All of this happened in the era of the famous Salem witch trials so it was in keeping with the times for the town folks to condemn her as a witch, a person who had sold her soul to the devil. Goody would continually be seen walking the high

Wellfleet cliffs gazing out to sea screaming curses into the winds on even the stormiest of Winter nights. Even today her ghost is said to walk the seaside cliffs of Cape Cod's outer shore near where Captain Black Bellamy's ship went down in 1717.

Was "Goody really a witch?

Could witch Goody have had a hand in brewing storms that shipwrecked more than two thousand ships and drowned uncounted thousands of mariners, including her lover captain Black Sam Bellamy, on the sandbars off South Wellfleet? There are those who believe she did.

On that fateful day in April 1717, at the height of the fierce storm, she was reportedly seen on the beach as the Whydah was sinking and sailors were drowning in the raging surf. People on the beach say they saw her high on the cliff shrieking thanks to the Devil for vengeance. All this happened off the South Wellfleet dunes near the lonely dilapidated shack in which Goody lived.

Goody Swallowed by a Whale?

"On April 22, 1751, she succumbed to the sea and was demolished by one of the whales off the coast. Further proof of this lies in the fact that when one of the whales was captured and cut open, inside they found Maria's red slippers."

Other tales have Goody riding upon the backs of whales with lanterns affixed to their tails in order to lure unsuspecting mariners onto the reefs and shoals of the outer cape referred to at the time as the "Graveyard of the Atlantic".

Lynne McIlveen Illustration

Goody swallowed by a whale

She is also supposed to have the power, as she was a witch, to conjure up storms and gales to the peril of seamen of the day. Storms such as the one that sank the Whydah and sent her scallywag lover to Davy Jones' locker.

Goody Hallett

Words and Music by Kiya Heartwood
Available for purchase at
www.wishingchair.com/music-group-7.html

They took the last man from the sea
But I swore I would never go
I knew she'd taken my love from me
Taken him down below

The first time I saw his raven hair
It was tied with a small dark bow
Four pistols he wore in his velvet
coat
I never saw a man so bold

He said my name is Samuel
Bellamy
Prince of all I obtain
Then he leaned and whispered in
my ear
Girl tell me your name

We tarried in the Wellfleet shops
And down in Eastham town
Then he asked my father if I could
wed
But my father turned him down

Say's there's talk you left
A wife and babe
Back in Cheltenham
But Sam he stared him in the eyes
He said, I'll take her and I can

Then Sam and Palgrave Williams
heard
Of galleons from Spain
Laden with gold and indigo
Lost in a hurricane

So Sam set his mind on treasure to
Salvage from the sea

He said, I'll go and find the tallest
ship
And I'll bring it back for thee

We said goodbye along the cliffs
And we made love fierce and wild
Then he took our plans
He took my soul
And he left me with his child.

Yes a boy was born
But soon he died
And they put me in their jail
They called me witch
And they called me whore
But I kept watch for his sails.

It was early that April morn
The sky was red and grey
But black that day soon became
That stole my love away

Yes her mast was cracked
Her hull was split
But I could hear the Whydah's bell
And she rang out the last
Sounds of hope
My true loves farewell

Now I walk the cliffs
And curse the sea
And every wind that blows
For the happiness we almost had
Now I will never know

92

The Beginning of Bellamy's Pirating Career

By all accounts Sam Bellamy was a rouge and a simple, blustering windbag of a man. His adventuresome spirit and gift of gab had enabled him to finance his quest for gold and also to seduce the loveliest girl on Cape Cod, Goody Hallett.

From the Cape, Bellamy sailed to the pirate haven of Newport, RI where he met Paulsgrave Williams. Paulsgrave came from a successful family. Bellamy was apparently successful in infecting Williams with gold fever and convinced Williams to contribute funds for his Caribbean adventure. The pair left Rhode Island together to begin their hunt for sunken Spanish treasure.

They searched for several months but, try as they would, had no luck finding any trace of sunken Spanish treasure as originally planned. Not wanting to return home as failures, together they decided that finding treasure on ships moving upon the surface of the water, rather than those sitting at the bottom of the sea, would be a much more profitable course of action.

Sailing to Newport, R.I.

They would make their fortune as pirates.

The two men met the notorious pirate Benjamin Hornigold and decided to join his crew of cut throats. It would appear that Captain Hornigold ran sort of a pirate training school as it was upon his ship that the later infamous Blackbeard also first sailed the Caribbean as a novice pirate.

Captain Hornigold was born in England and accordingly would only attack French and Spanish ships, not English ships. In June 1716, his crew revolted against him because they wanted to attack an English ship.

The crew voted Samuel Bellamy and Paulsgrave Williams as the new Captain and Quartermaster, respectively.

Bellamy and his crew plundered more than fifty ships making him one of the most successful pirates of the era. He was now known as "Black Bellamy" or "Black Sam". Perhaps his nickname, "Black", was a reference to his preference for the expensive black clothes he always wore. Dressed all in black, and with four dueling pistols around his waist, he was a formidable figure.

Black Sam was a fine strategist. He would employ two ships in his raids. The first, his flagship, was armed with many cannons but relatively slow. The second, captained by Paulsgrave Williams, was lightly armed but fast. With this combination of assets Black Sam was able to coordinated attacks and capture ships with relative ease without damaging them.

Jolly Roger flown by Black Sam

With his ship loaded with this treasure and the booty plundered from more than fifty other ships, Black Bellamy and his crew decided to retire from pirating. They were now richer than their wildest imaginations could ever have imagined.

Black Sam and his crew set a Northerly course and headed for home. For some home was in New England; for others, home was further away in England. Where was Black Sam heading? Was he going home to the wife and child left in England, or was he returning, as promised, to the young farm girl he seduced on Cape Cod?

Some, who believe he was returning for the Cape's Goody Hallett, will refer to Black Sam Bellamy as the "Romantic Pirate." If returning to Goody was his plan, perhaps those in England would call him a different name.

On April 26, near Cape Cod, *Whydah* and its crew of 148 souls ran into an intense late winter storm. Despite Herculean efforts of the crew, the *Whydah* struck the bar off South Wellfleet near what is now Marconi Beach in the Cape Cod National Seashore Park and sank as raging surf tore her to pieces.

People along the beach watching the tragic scene reported hearing and seeing "Goody" Hallett high upon the dunes screaming thanks to the Devil for vengeance.

The next day a search for survivors and perhaps treasure, revealed only bits and pieces of floating remains of the once proud flagship *Whydah* and her crew.

Only two survived the *Wydah's* sinking and live to tell the stories of Captain Black Sam Bellamy: an Indian pilot and Thomas Davis, a Welsh carpenter. It was Davis' vivid account of the shipwreck that was passed from generation to generation to become part of Cape Cod folklore. Essentially all that is known of Black Sam the pirate comes from stories recounted by Thomas Davis. Thomas Davis was jailed, tried, and acquitted of piracy.

The Encyclopedia Americana" says of Samuel Bellamy,

> *"...a notorious pirate, was wrecked in his ship, the "Whidah", of 23 guns and 130 men, off Wellfleet, on Cape Cod, in April 1717, after having captured several vessels on the coast and an indecisive engagement with a French ship proceeding to Quebec.*
>
> *Only one Indian and one Englishman escaped of his crew. Six of the pirates, who had been run ashore when drunk a few days previous, by the captain of the captured vessel, were hung in Boston in November 1717. "Black Sam," as he was known by then, was never seen again, nor was his body ever recovered."*

In 1984 the wreck of the *Whydah* was discovered by Barry Clifford of Tisbury, Massachusetts in the shallow waters off of Wellfleet. The value of the treasure is estimated by some to approximate $400 million dollars.

Prior to the discovery of the ship's bell with the name *Whydah* the name of the ship was believed to be spelled "*Whidah.*"

Was Captain Black Bellamy Tricked into Eternity?

In the spring of 1717, Bellamy and Williams are reported to have captured seven ships on their return trip to Cape Cod. Approaching the Cape, Consort Captain Williams, aboard sloop *Mary Anne*, was dropped off at Block Island, an island just south of Cape Cod, to visit family

Bellamy following pilot ship

The weather was deteriorating as Bellamy's fleet continued north to the Cape. One of the ships was a captured wine carrying sloop captained by a native Cape Codder. Legend has Bellamy promising this captain the return of his ship if he would lead the fleet into the safe harbor at Provincetown

He was made this remarkable promise because he had extensive knowledge of the treacherous, shoaled waters off the Outer Cape known as the graveyard of the North Atlantic. The bones of literally thousands of hapless ships lay upon its sandy ocean bottom.

A lantern was hung in the rigging so that Bellamy and his flagship the *Whydah* would be able to follow in the darkness of the moonless night.

Caught in the death grip of the storm

The wily Cape Cod captain apparently had other plans. He allowed the pirates left onboard to guard the prize to become drunk on the cargo of wine the ship carried. Then, with his captors thus incapacitated, he tossed a burning tar barrel overboard for the *Whydah* to follow into eternity via the sandy treacherous sandy shoals of the Outer Cape while he sailed safely into Provincetown harbor.

Pirates from William's *Mary Anne* (Williams was on shore visiting his mother) was wrecked in the storm were caught where they washed ashore in Provincetown, put on trial and hanged in Boston. Thoreau mentions the *Whydah* tragedy in his book, *Cape Cod*. He wrote,``A storm coming on, their whole fleet was wrecked, and more than a hundred dead bodies lay along the shore." The shore he references is Marconi Beach in Wellfleet.

I'm from the Government and I'm Here to Help

News of shipwrecked treasure traveled very fast. Within days officials in Boston sent a ship to the Cape to "protect the government's interests." In other words, to confiscate the treasure. Posters were immediately put up warning that anyone found with shipwreck goods would face a severe penalty.

The government's men scoured the beaches, searched barns, sheds, yards and houses for miles around attempting to uncover booty of any kind. They confiscated several wagonloads of goods but no serious treasure was uncovered.

Prior to the arrival of the government ship, hundreds of men from all across the Cape had scoured the beach of anything of value. Reportedly the only thing left for the government team to recover was the pirate ship's anchor cable.

Centuries later the state of Massachusetts would claim joint ownership of the *Whydah* and demand to regulate the salvage of any artifacts and treasure it might contain.

The difference this time was that lawyers were dispatched to a court room to confiscate the treasure and not to a ship.

After several years the suit was settled in favor of the treasure hunter Barry Clifford, the man who had invested fifteen years and countless dollars in order to find the treasure ship.

Legend of "Goody's" Buried Treasure

Some legends say that "Goody" had retrieved a chest of pirate gold from the surf that stormy night and buried it somewhere in the Wellfleet dunes. Because "Goody" Hallett had "lost her mind" she apparently forgot where she buried the treasure for she continued to eek out a meager living until the day she died. If she did bury treasure, she kept the whereabouts a secret and took the location with her to her grave.

Another story of buried treasure has the two survivors Thomas Davis and John Julian visiting the house of Samuel Hardings in Wellfleet on the night of the disaster. According to the story... the next morning, the three men hitched up Hardings' wagon and retrieved several wagonloads of the wreck's treasure from the beach. They secreted it in Hardings' barn before hiding it more securely, perhaps by burying the fortune somewhere on the Harding property.

About a week after the wreck, Governor Shute sent a Captain Cypian Southack to the Cape to recover as much of the pirate treasure as possible. He searched some private homes and commandeered some of the salvaged good but found no trace of the cargo.

Is there still buried gold somewhere in the Wellfleet dunes? Perhaps the treasure still lies beneath the sand where Goody buried it waiting to be uncovered or has it already been found?

It is rumored that Sam Bellamy's ghost still walks Wellfleet's cliffs and dunes in search of his lost treasure. To this day gold coins can be found washed up on Wellfleet's beach after big storms.

The Only Treasure Laden Pirate Ship Ever Recovered

Lays Mere Yards off a Cape Cod Beach

The *Whydah Gally* (commonly known simply as the *Whydah* or *Whidah*, sometimes, written as *Whidaw*, or *Whida)* was a fully rigged galley ship that was originally built as a slave ship for the Atlantic slave trade. On the return leg of its second voyage of the Triangle Trade, it began a new role in the Golden Age of Piracy, when it was captured by the pirate Captain "Black Sam" Bellamy, and refitted as his flagship.

The Whydah Gally (1716–1717)

Two months later, on April 26, 1717, the ship ran aground and capsized during a strong gale force storm off of Cape Cod, taking Bellamy, 143 of his crew, and over 4.5 tons of gold and silver with it, leaving only two survivors to tell its tale.

The *Whydah* and its treasure eluded discovery for over 260 years until 1984, when the wreck was found – under just 14 feet of water and 5 feet of sand – becoming the first authenticated pirate shipwreck to ever be discovered.

Slave ship

The *Whydah Gally* was commissioned in 1715 in London, England by independent merchants. A square-rigged three masted ship, it measured 102 ft in length, with a tonnage rating at 300 tons burthen, and could travel at speeds up to 13 knots (15 mph).

Christened *Whydah* after the West African slave trading kingdom of Quidah (pronounced *WIH-dah*), the vessel was configured as a heavily armed trading and transport ship for use in the Atlantic slave trade. It set out for its maiden voyage in early 1716, carrying goods from England to exchange for slaves in West Africa.

Jolly Roger

After traveling down West Africa through modern-day Gambia and Senegal to Nigeria and arrived at Benin where its namesake port was located.

It left Africa with 367 captives, gold, jewellry, and ivory aboard, and traveled to the Caribbean, where it traded the 312 surviving captives for precious metals, sugar, indigo, rum, and medicinal ingredients, which were to then be transported back to England. Fitted with a standard complement of eighteen six-pound cannon, which could be increased to a total of twenty-eight in time of war, the *Whydah* represented one of the most advanced weapons systems of the time.

Pirate Ship

In late February 1717, the *Whydah*, under the command of Captain Lawrence Prince, was navigating the Windward Passage between Cuba and Hispaniola when it was attacked by pirates led by "Black Sam" Bellamy. At the time of the *Whydah's* capture, Bellamy was in possession of two vessels, the 26-gun galley *Sultana* and the converted 10-gun sloop *Mary Anne*. After a three-day chase, Prince surrendered his ship near the Bahamas with only a minimal exchange of cannon fire.

Bellamy decided to take the *Whydah* as his new flagship. Several of its crew remained with their ship and joined the pirate gang. Pirate recruitment was most effective among the unemployed, escaped bondsmen, and transported criminals, as the high seas made for an instant leveling of class distinctions.

In a gesture of goodwill toward Captain Prince who had surrendered without a struggle—and who in any case may have been favorably known by reputation to the pirate crew— Bellamy gave the *Sultana* to Prince, along with £20 in silver and gold.

"...they spread a large black flag, with a Death's Head and Bones across, and gave chase to Cap't Prince under the same colors." – Thomas Baker (Bellamy's crew) on Whydah pursuit

---

The *Whydah* was then fitted with 10 additional cannons by its new captain, and 150 members of Bellamy's crew were detailed to man the vessel. They cleared the top deck of the pilot's cabin, removed the slave barricade, and got rid of other features that made her top heavy.

Bellamy and his crew then sailed on to the Carolinas and headed north along the eastern coastline of the American colonies, aiming for the central coast of Maine, looting or capturing additional vessels on the way. At some point during his possession of the *Whydah*, Bellamy loaded an additional 30+ cannons below decks, possibly as ballast. Two cannons recovered by underwater explorer Barry Clifford in August 2009 weighed 800 and 1,500 pounds respectively.

> *They could not wipe out the North-East gales*
> *Nor what those gales set free —*
> *The pirate ships with their close-reefed sails,*
> *Leaping from sea to sea.*

—Rudyard Kipling, *"The Pirates of New England"*

Accounts differ as to the destination of the *Whydah* during its last few days. Some evidence exists to support local Cape Cod legend: the *Whydah* was headed for what is now Provincetown Harbor at the tip of Cape Cod, so that Bellamy could visit his love, Maria Hallett – the "Witch of Wellfleet". Others blame the *Whydah's* route on navigator error. In any case, on April 26, 1717, near Chatham, Massachusetts, the *Whydah* approached a thick, gray fog bank rolling across the water – signaling inclement weather ahead.

Shipwreck

That weather turned into a violent nor'easter, a storm with gale force winds out of the east and northeast, which forced the vessel dangerously close to the breaking waves along the shoals of Cape Cod. The ship was eventually driven aground at Wellfleet, Massachusetts. At midnight she hit a sandbar in 14 feet of water about 500 feet from the coast of what **is** now Marconi Beach.

Map showing the location of the wrecked *Whvdah*

Pummeled by 70 mph winds and 30-to-40 ft waves, the main mast snapped, pulling the ship into about 30 ft of water, where she violently capsized.

The 60+ cannon on board ripped through the overturned decks of the ship and quickly broke it apart, scattering parts of the ship over a 4-mile length of coast. One of the two surviving members of Bellamy's crew, Thomas Davis, testified in his subsequent trial that "*In a quarter of an hour after the ship struck, the Mainmast was carried by the board, and in the Morning she was beat to pieces.*"

By morning, hundreds of Cape Cod's notorious wreckers (locally known as "moon-cussers") were already plundering the remains. Hearing of the shipwreck, then-governor Samuel Shute dispatched Captain Cyprian Southack, a local salvager and cartographer, to recover "*Money, Bullion, Treasure, Goods and Merchandizes taken out of the said Ship.*"

When Southack reached the wreck on May 3rd, he found that part of the ship was still visible breaching the water's surface, but that much of the ship's wreckage was scattered along a long stretch of shoreline.

On a map that he made of the wreck site, Southack reported that he had buried 102 of the 144 *Whydah* crew and captives lost in the sinking (though

Moon-cussers at work

technically they were buried by the town coroner, who surprised Southack by handing him the bill and demanding payment).

According to surviving members of the crew – two from the *Whydah* and seven from the *"Wine Ship"*, another of Bellamy's fleet which reached the safety of Provincetown Harbor. At the time of its sinking, the *Whydah* carried from four and a half to five tons of silver, gold, gold dust, and jewelry, which had been divided equally into 180 50-pound sacks and stored in-between the ship's decks.

Though Southack did salvage some nearly worthless items from the ship, little of the massive treasure hoard was recovered. Southack would write in his account of his findings, that, "The riches, with the guns, would be buried in the sand. With that, the exact location of the ship, its riches and its guns were lost, and eventually came to be thought of as nothing more than legend.

Survivors

Including the seven men aboard the "Wine Ship", nine of Bellamy's crew survived the wrecking of the *Whydah* and *Mary Anne*. They were all captured quickly, however, and on October 18, 1717, six were tried in Boston for piracy and robbery. The following were found guilty and sentenced to death by hanging: John Brown of Jamaica, Thomas Baker and Hendrick Quintor

of the Netherlands; Peter Cornelius Hoof of Sweden; John Shaun of France; and Simon van der Vorst of New York.

Carpenters Thomas South and Thomas Davis, who were tried separately, had been conscripted by Bellamy – forced to choose between a life of piracy or death. Therefore, they were acquitted of all charges and spared the gallows. The last survivor was a 16-year-old Miskito Indian named John Julian – who was a

Pirate John Julian

skilled navigator, and also the *Whydah's* pilot. He was not tried, but instead was sold into slavery after his capture.

On November 15, 1717, the famous Puritan minister Cotton Mather accompanied the six condemned men as they were rowed across Boston Harbor to Charlestown. All six men confessed and repented in the presence of Mather, but they were still hanged.

"The riches, with the guns, would be buried in the sand."

Recovery

The wreck of the *Whydah* was discovered in 1984 by underwater explorer Barry Clifford, who relied heavily on Southack's 1717 map of the wreck site – a modern-day, true-to-life "pirate treasure map" leading to what was at that time a discovery of unprecedented proportions. That the *Whydah* had eluded discovery for over 260 years became even more surprising when the wreck was found under just 14 feet of water and 5 feet of sand.

The ship's location has been the site of extensive underwater archaeology, and more than 200,000 individual pieces have since been retrieved.

One major find in the fall of 1985 was the ship's bell, inscribed with the words "THE WHYDAH GALLY 1716". With that, the *Whydah* became the first ever pirate shipwreck with its

Gold from the pirate ship *Whydah*

identity having been established and authenticated beyond a shadow of a doubt.

Work on the site by Clifford's dive team continues on an annual basis. Selected artifacts from the wreck are displayed at Expedition *Whydah* Sea-Lab & Learning Center (The *Whydah* Pirate Museum) in Provincetown, Massachusetts. A selection of the artifacts is also on a tour across the United States under the sponsorship of the National Geographic Society.

Archaeological evidence

As bits and pieces of the pirates' weapons, clothing, gear, and other possessions have been plucked from the wreck, researchers have logged the locations where they were found, then gently stowed them in water-filled vats to prevent drying. The artifacts have revealed a picture of the pirates quite unlike their popular image as thuggish white men with sabers.

The bell is inscribed
"THE WHYDAH GALLEY 1716"

The abundance of metal buttons, cuff links, collar stays, rings, neck chains, and square belt buckles scattered on the sea floor shows that the pirates were far more sophisticated—even dandyish—in their dress than was previously thought. In an age of austere Puritanism and rigid class hierarchy, this too was an act of defiance—similar in spirit, perhaps, to today's rock stars.

The most common items found in the wreck haven't been eye patches and rum bottles but bits of bird shot and musket balls, designed to clear decks of defenders but not to damage ships. The pirates, it seems, preferred close-quarters fighting with antipersonnel weapons over destructive cannon battles. Among the custom-made weapons that have been recovered are dozens of homemade hand grenades: hollow, baseball-size iron spheres, which were filled with gunpowder and plugged shut. A gunpowder fuse was run through the plug's center, to be lit moments before the grenade was tossed onto the deck of a victim ship. Pirates didn't want to sink a ship; they wanted to capture and rob it.

The Boy Pirate

Famously, the youngest known member of the Whydah's crew was a boy aged approximately 11 years of age, named John King. Young John actually chose to join the crew on his own initiative the previous November, when Bellamy captured the ship on which he and his mother were passengers. He was reported to have been so insistent that he threatened to hurt his mother if he wasn't allowed to join Bellamy.

Among the *Whydah* artifacts recovered by Barry Clifford were a small, black, leather shoe, together with a silk stocking and fibula bone, later determined to be that of a child between 8 and 11 years old – confirming yet another "pirate tale" as fact.

Shoe and Stocking of the Whydah's Youngest Pirate

Reaction

A museum exhibition entitled "Real Pirates: The Untold Story of The *Whydah* from Slave Ship to Pirate Ship" toured the United States from 2007 to 2012. Venues included: Cincinnati Museum Center, Cincinnati, OH; The Franklin Institute, Philadelphia, PA; The Field Museum, Chicago, IL; Nauticus, Norfolk, VA; St. Louis, MO; Houston, TX; and the Science Museum of Minnesota, St. Paul, MN.

In one instance, the *Whydah's* brief participation in the Atlantic slave trade was a source of controversy. The Museum of Science and Industry in Tampa, Florida announced the exhibit and linked it to the 2007 release of *Pirates of the Caribbean: At World's End*. After being criticized for trivializing the ship's role in slavery while glorifying its role in piracy, the museum canceled the exhibit.

Palgrave Williams
Rhode Island's "Royal" Pirate

Palgrave Williams served as Black Sam Bellamy's quartermaster, and became Consort Captain of the sloop *Mary Anne,* in Bellamy's small fleet of pirate raiders.

Born in Rhode Island, the 39 year old Williams was a successful and very wealthy goldsmith from a prestigious family. When he met Samuel Bellamy in the Fall of 1715, Sam apparently infected him with "Treasure Fever." Soon after

Palgrave Williams in Battle

their meeting the pair headed off to the Caribbean to retrieve sunken Spanish treasure.

Search as they might they were unable to discover any sunken Spanish treasure so, rather than return home empty handed, they turned to piracy. In just a year of raiding Williams and Bellamy plundered more than 50 ships on the Caribbean and Atlantic.

He, like Bellamy left his wife and children to begin a great treasure hunting adventure. Why would a very rich family man give it all up to fund a complete stranger on chance that treasure ships wrecked off the coast of Florida could be found? Perhaps he suffered from a seventeenth century form of mid-life crisis.

Roots to Royalty and American Presidents

Williams could trace his roots to one of England's great families, the Mowbrays, who in the Middle Ages lived on the Isle of Axholme, Lincolnshire. It is through this family that British leaders, American Presidents, Hollywood stars, the present Queen of England and, Diana, Princess of Wales can claim to have a pirate on their family tree.

Royalty on the family tree

Williams is reportedly related to: Anne Boleyn, Elizabeth I, Sir Winston Churchill, Audrey Hepburn, George Washington, Thomas Jefferson and the presidents Bush, two wives of Henry VIII, Pocahontas and the Duchess from *Alice in Wonderland*.

First a Quartermaster

Palgrave was elected quartermaster by the crew, as was the custom of the day. The quartermaster's job was to protect the crew's interests, and to act as a check-and-balance on the power of the captain. Next to the captain, he was the most important person aboard a pirate ship.

It is the duty of a quartermaster to run the day to day operations of the ship, sort of a Chief Operating Officer or COO of the sea. It is his responsibility to:

- manage ship's bookwork (therefore must be literate)
- assign work details,
- settle quarrels,
- maintain battle readiness,
- punish minor infractions,
- apportion provisions,
- assign battle stations,
- ensure booty is shared appropriately

A person elected to this position was respected by the pirates as a trustworthy, intelligent and responsible man. It was not unusual for a quartermaster to next be elected captain by the crew.

Then Bellamy's Consort Captain,

His first command was as Consort Captain of the sloop *Mary Anne,* a well-armed sloop, her hull still gaily painted the blue and yellow colors of her original French owners.

A Consort Captain is a commander who commands a vessel accompanying another, such as Black Sam's flagship the *Whydah*.

Captains Bellamy and Williams would co-ordinate their attacks upon their prey with the agile *Mary Anne* cornering the prey and Black Sam's larger ship, bristling with scores of cannon, would intimidate essentially all their conquests into surrendering without a fight.

Ship similar to the Mary Anne

His captives later reported that even while pirating for months in the tropics, Williams continued to wear his powdered gentleman's wig.

When the fleet sailed north from the Bahamas in the spring of 1717, Williams would take a detour that saved his life. He debarked at Block Island, Rhode Island, to visit his mother and sisters there and planned to rejoin the *Whydah* later. The *Mary Anne* continued northward and would soon be shipwrecked, along with the *Whydah,* off the coast of Cape Cod.

Williams and Bellamy planned to rendezvous at Damariscove Island, Maine on or around May 20. Williams would visit his mother and sisters on Block Island, stay ashore for a day or two, probably disposed of some of his plunder and meet up with Bellamy in Maine.

During March Bellamy and Williams captured four more vessels while off Virginia. One of these, a sloop the name of which is unknown, was added to the small fleet which now numbered four ships including the "Wine Ship."

Since both the *Whydah* and the *Mary Anne* were lost in the storm and the Wine Ship made the safety of Provincetown Harbor, and Williams is reported to have gone to Maine to await Bellamy, one must calculate that this nameless fourth ship was William's transport.

After visiting he then made his way to Damariscove Island, and wait for Bellamy to join him there. After two weeks word arrived that his friend, Sam Bellamy, was dead and the *Whydah*, the treasure and all hands save two were lost. With a

Pirates attack Merchant ship

heavy heart he set sail for the pirate base at New Providence. Before he left New England however, he is reported to have plundered two more merchant ships off of Cape Cod.

He was at New Providence in February 1718 when Vincent Pearse of HMS *Phoenix* visited the island, but would flee to Africa prior to the arrival of the new governor Woodes Rogers.

He was last seen off Sierra Leone in April 1720, serving as an officer aboard a pirate ship commanded by the notorious French pirate and fellow "Flying Gang" member, Olivier La Buse.

The End and a New Beginning

Williams would retire from piracy for a short time but, longing for the exciting life of a pirate, he went back to sea within a year. He would continue to plunder and raid innocent merchant ships for several more years. Then in 1723, at the age of 45, he retired a second and final time.

Williams is said to have settled down with a new wife and name and began a second family. Unlike most pirates of the day, he escaped the gallows and died an uneventful death.

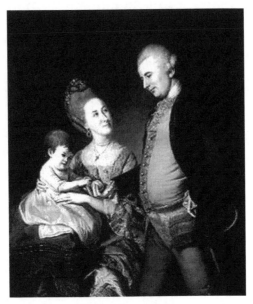

Retired from piracy

Blackbeard the Pirate

Edward Teach a/k/a Blackbeard was an English sailor whose piracy career began in 1716 and ended on November 22, 1718 in a bloody battle off Ocracoke Inlet, North Carolina. He terrorized shipping from the Caribbean to New England at the height of the period known as the "Golden Age of Piracy."

Blackbeard

Before turning to piracy, Teach had gallantly served England as a privateer in the "Queen Anne's War" that ended in 1713.

He learned the tricks of the pirate's trade from pirate Benjamin Hornigold. Hornigold rewarded Teach by gifting him with a ship they had hijacked. Teach renamed this craft "Queen Anne's Revenge" and outfitted her with 40 cannon and a crew of 300 and was off to pirate on his own.

He cruised the Caribbean and the coastal waters of the American colonies as far north as Maine in New England attacking shipping, stealing cargos, torturing passengers and crews and leaving havoc in his wake.

Having a fearful persona and a reputation of being heartless was as important to the success of a pirate as were the number of cannons aboard his fleet. Pirates used symbolism along with their actions to instill terror into the hearts of all whom they approached.

Not all pirate flags were skulls and cross bones as Blackbeard's flag or "Jolly Roger" illustrates. Blackbeard's flag depicting a heart dripping blood while a devil skeleton held an hourglass and spear, was designed to strike fear in his victims. It apparently worked as many captains reportedly gave up their ships without firing a shot when they spied his "Jolly Roger".

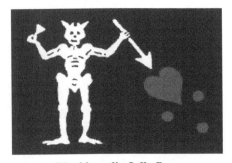

Blackbeard's Jolly Roger

Blackbeard was a very large man who stood 6' 6" tall, with long, thick black hair and beard and wore a constant scowl upon his face. His natural wild eyed appearance was indeed frightening. To heighten his fearsome appearance, Blackbeard would go into battle with lighted hemp tapers in his beard and hair. He was a frightening sight indeed and, to many, appeared to be some kind of supernatural devil.

Fearsome figure

Blackbeard would arm himself with an arsenal of weapons in preparation for battle. He would carry several loaded pistols on cords around his neck and a few more in his bandolier. The multiple pistols were an advantage when attacking as pistols of the day were single shot weapons. In addition to carrying multiple pistols he also would arm himself with several swords, daggers and knives.

His fearsome image and reputation, which he cultivated, has carried over to this day as the name Blackbeard still conjures up visions of a ruthless pirate.

Blackbeard's buried treasure in New England

The Isles of Shoals are a group of nine islands located six miles off the coast of Maine and New Hampshire. These islands lie right in the path of shipping coming from and going to Europe following the warm currents of the Gulf Stream.

Malaga, the smallest of the islands being only 300 by 500 feet, is said to have been named by Spanish mariners. In the 1820s four bars of silver found on the island by captain Samuel Haley were sold by him to fund the construction of a breakwater to connect Malaga with the larger Smuttynose island.

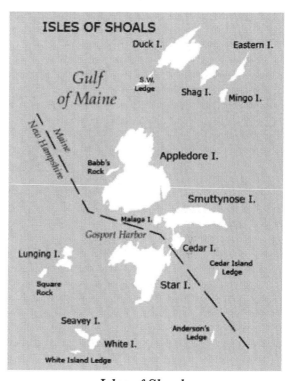

Isles of Shoals

Smuttynose is also where the Spanish bark "Sagunto" sank on January, 14 1813. All hands on board died. Fourteen were found over the next few days, some having crawled ashore only to meet their maker as a frozen corpse. No treasure or cargo has ever been reported recovered.

Blackbeard took fourteen wives and fathered forty children. He is said to have honeymooned on Smuttynose with his thirteenth before leaving her to guard his treasure while awaiting his return. One legend reports that Blackbeard buried treasure on a half-moon shaped beach somewhere on Smuttynose Island.

117

He never did return and his bride's ghost is reportedly still seen on the island occasionally. Is she still guarding the location of the treasure or is her spirit awaiting the return of her black hearted lover?

Blackbeard buries his treasure

Lunging island is the location most strongly rumored to still hold Blackbeard's buried treasure. The treasure is said to be secreted in a cave long since collapsed and covered by nearly 300 years of storm and tide.

The end of a career

Blackbeard bid his newest wife and treasure farewell and sailed south to his favorite hunting grounds off the Carolinas. It was here he was to marry his fourteenth wife, Mary Ormond of Bath, North Carolina and meet his maker in waters near Ocracoke Village, North Carolina

Blackbeard found the inland and coastal waterways ideal conditions within which he would conduct his trade. The confined waterway, with its shallow coves and inlets, were ideal for hunting commercial ships and avoiding capture by larger deep drafted naval vessels.

Life was good here for the pirates. Not only were physical conditions conducive to pirating but, in addition, Blackbeard had bribed the colonial governor, Charles Eden, to leave them alone in return for a share of the booty.

At one point Blackbeard had several ships in his pirate fleet and commanded more than seven hundred men. He terrorized the Carolina

Blackbeard's head on the bow sprit

coast for eighteen months including a blockade of Charleston.

His career would come to an end when irate Carolinians appealed in desperation to the then governor of Virginia, Governor Spotswood, for aid. Spotswood engaged Royal Navy Lieutenant Robert Maynard to assemble a task force and put an end to Blackbeard's reign of terror.

On November 22, 1718, Maynard's two shallow drafted sloops *Ranger* and *Jane* with sixty-two men found Blackbeard anchored in Ocracoke Inlet preparing his newest ship *Adventurer* for battle.

Blackbeard in battle

Athough outmanned by almost four to one Blackbeard came close to winning the battle. However, Blackbeard was fooled into leading a charge aboard Maynard's vessel as Maynard had hidden his main force below decks thereby luring Blackbeard's lesser numbers into a trap. Maynard and his men emerged and proceeded to cut down the outnumbered pirates one by one.

The fight ended when Teach fell. He was shot five times and stabbed more than twenty and finally stopped fighting when he finally was decapitated. His body was thrown overboard and legend holds the body swam around the ship seven times before finally sinking in the channel that now bears his name, Teach's Hole.

Teach's head was placed as a trophy on the bowsprit of Maynard's ship. In order to claim his reward Maynard was required to submit Blackbeard's head to governor Spotswood as proof. Later, the head was hung from a pike in Bath, North Carolina where it stayed for many years.

Blackbeard was very proficient at self promotion. He wanted his persona and reputation strike fear into all. As example, one legend reports Blackbeard as blustering that he shot his own first mate, because "if he didn't shoot one or two [crewmen] now and then, they'd forget who he was." His self promotion was more successful than he could have ever imagined. Three hundred years later his reputation and giant sized legend continues larger than ever with scores of books, movies, television programs produced memorializing him for the ages

.

Blackbeard

Captain Howell Davis

His piratical career lasted just 11 months, from 11 July 1718 to
19 June 1719, when he was ambushed and killed. His ships
were the *Cadogan, Buck, Saint James,* and *Rover.* Davis
captured 15 known English and French ships.

Joined with the "Flying Gang"

Born in Wales, Davis started out in piracy on 11 July 1718
when the slave
ship *Cadogan,* on
which he was
serving as a mate,
was captured by
the pirate Edward
England. Deciding
to join the pirates,
Davis was given
command of the
Cadogan and set
out for Brazil on 18
July 1718.

Captain Howell Davis

However, his crew mutinied and sailed to Barbados instead.
Here Davis was imprisoned on the charge of piracy, but was
eventually released and sought shelter in the pirate den of New
Providence. With New Providence being cleaned out by
Governor Woodes Rogers, Davis left on the sloop *Buck* and
conspired with six other crew members who were "Flying Gang"
members, including Thomas Anstis and Walter Kennedy, to
take over the vessel off Martinique. Davis was elected captain
and conducted raids from his base at Coxon's Hole.

Subsequently, he crossed the Atlantic to terrorize shipping in
the Cape Verde Islands. One of the prizes he took there became
the new flagship of Davis' pirate fleet, the 26-gun *Saint James.*
He then formed a partnership with a French pirate Olivier
Levasseur, known as *La Buse,* and another pirate captain,
Thomas Cocklyn, which lasted until they fell out in a drunken
argument. Transferring to the 32-gun *Rover,* Davis sailed south
and captured more rich prizes off the Gold Coast.

Tutors Bartholomew "Black Bart" Roberts

One of his prisoners was fellow Welshman Bartholomew Roberts, who was destined to become even more famous as a pirate. He was third mate on the slave ship *Princess*, under Captain Abraham Plumb. In early June that year the *Princess* was anchored at Anambah which is situated along the Gold Coast of West Africa (present-day Ghana), when his ship was captured by pirates. The pirates were in two vessels, the *Royal Rover* and the *Royal James*, and were led by Captain Howell Davis.

Davis quickly discovered Roberts' abilities as a navigator and took to consulting him. He was also able to confide to Roberts information in Welsh, thereby keeping it hidden from the rest of the crew. Roberts is said to have been reluctant to become a pirate at first, but soon came to see the advantages of this new lifestyle.

His Trickery and Deception Backfire

A clever and charming man as he was, Davis pretended to be a legitimate privateer to deceive the commander of a Royal African Company slaving fort in Gambia. After capturing the commander at a welcoming dinner, Davis held him for ransom and gained 2,000 pounds in gold.

He once seized a more powerful French vessel by flying a black pirate flag from another large but lightly armed ship he had recently taken. The French ship quickly surrendered, thinking she was outgunned.

Davis ambushed and shot dead

However, when he tried to pretend he was a Royal Navy pirate hunter in order to kidnap the governor of the Portuguese island of Príncipe, the governor saw through it.

Davis was invited to call at the fort for a glass of wine. On the way there, the pirates were ambushed and Davis shot dead on 19 June 1719. Bartholomew Roberts was elected to succeed him and raided the island in retaliation later that night.

Pirates raiding an island town

Olivier Levasseur (La Buse)

He was nicknamed *La Buse* (The Buzzard) or *La Bouche* (*The Mouth*). He was also known as Louis Labous, La Bouse, La Bouche, and La Buze, He was renowned for the speed and ruthlessness with which he always attacked his enemies.

Born at Calais, France during the Nine Years' War (1688–97) to a wealthy bourgeois family, he received an excellent education and became an officer in the French Navy. During the War of the Spanish Succession (1701–1714), he procured a Letter of Marque from King Louis XIV and became a privateer for the French crown.

Olivier Levasseur

When the war ended he was ordered to return home with his ship, but instead joined Benjamin Hornigold's pirate company in 1716. La Buse proved himself a good leader and shipmate, even though he had a scar across one eye that limited his sight.

By 1716, when he was the Consort Captain of Benjamin Hornigold's pirate sloop *Postillion* and operating along with Sam Bellamy and Paulsgraves Williams. After weeks of successful pillaging in the vicinity of Cuba, La Buse, Williams and Bellamy had a falling out with Hornigold. They left Hornigold and embarked on a successful cruise to the Eastern Caribbean in the fall and early winter of 1716. The three appear to have become close partners and allies.

La Buse, Williams and Bellamy continued to the coast of South America where they captured a large "ship of force." They appeared seven months later off the New England coast in this 26-gun ship crewed by some 200 men, making La Buse one of the most formidable pirates at the time.

He captured several small vessels crossing the Gulf of Maine before vanishing for several months. It is possible that he was the pirate who built a fortified base in Machias, Maine and raided vessels off Newfoundland, actions that some have attributed to Sam Bellamy.

In 1719 he operated together with Howell Davis and Thomas Cocklyn for a time. In 1720, they attacked the slaver port of Ouidah, on the coast of Benin, reducing the local fortress to ruins. Later that year, he was shipwrecked in the Mozambique Channel and stranded on the island of Anjouan, one of the Comores. His bad eye had become completely blind by now so he began wearing an eye patch.

Collected $13 Million and Marooned Captain English

From 1720 onwards he launched his raids from a base on the island of Sainte-Marie, just off the Madagascar coast, together with pirates John Taylor and Edward England, (probably planning to capture one of the Great Mughal's heavily armed but also heavily treasure laden pilgrim ships to Mecca). They first plundered the *Laccadives*, and sold the loot to Dutch traders for £75,000 ($13,000,000 in 2013 dollars after adjusting for inflation). La Buse

Captain English Marooned by La Buse and Taylor

and Taylor eventually got tired of England's abrasive personality and marooned him on the island of Mauritius.

They then perpetrated one of piracy's greatest exploits: the capture of the Portuguese great galleon *Nossa Senhora do Cabo (Our Lady of the Cape)* or *Virgem Do Cabo (The Virgin of the Cape)*, loaded full of treasures belonging to the Bishop of Goa, also called the Patriarch of the East Indies, as well as the

126

Viceroy of Portugal, who were both on board returning home to Lisbon.

The pirates were able to board the vessel without firing a single broadside, because the *Cabo* had been damaged in a storm, and to avoid capsizing the crew had dumped all of its 72 cannon overboard, and then anchored off Réunion Island to undergo repairs. (This incident would later be used by Robert Louis Stevenson in his novel "Treasure Island" where the galleon is referred to as *The Viceroy of the Indies* in the account given by his famed fictional character Long John Silver).

Fantastic Amount of Treasure Seized

The booty consisted of bars of gold and silver, dozens of boxes full of golden Guineas, diamonds, pearls, silk, art and religious objects from the Se Cathedral in Goa, including the *Flaming Cross of Goa* made of pure gold, inlaid with diamonds, rubies and emeralds. The cross was so heavy, that it required 3 men to carry it over to La Buse's ship.

Mound of Pirate's Gold, Silver and Jewels

In fact, the treasure was so huge (estimated $803,600,000 in 2013) that the pirates did not bother to rob the people on board, something they normally would have done.

When the loot was divided, each pirate received at least $50,000 in golden Guineas ($8,100,000 adjusted for inflation to 2013), as well as 42 diamonds each. La Buse and Taylor split the remaining gold, silver, and other objects, with La Buse taking the golden cross.

In 1724, La Buse sent a negotiator to the governor on the island of Bourbon (today Réunion), to discuss an amnesty that had been offered to all pirates in the Indian Ocean who would give up their practice. However, the French government wanted a large part of the stolen loot back, so La Buse decided to avoid the amnesty and settled down in secret on the Seychelles archipelago. Eventually he was captured near Fort Dauphin, Madagascar.

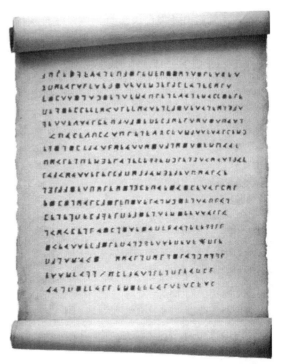

A replica of La Buse's secret message

He was then taken to Saint-Denis, Réunion and hanged for piracy at 5 p.m. on 7 July 1730. Legend says that when he stood on the gallows with a piece of black cloth covering his eyes, he wore a necklace that contains a17 line coded message of directions to where he had hidden his vast fortune. He threw it into the crowd who were there to witness his execution and shouted, "Find my treasure who could interpret it for you!" Today, his grave is a popular tourist site and his treasure is still un-found.

Thomas Cocklyn

He was an English pirate, known primarily for his association and partnership with Howell Davis and Oliver La Buse. He was reportedly elected captain "due to his brutality and ignorance" when first sailing from New Providence in 1717.

Pirates attacking from small boats

On April 1, 1719, Cocklyn was a participant in the capture of the West African bound English slave ship the *Bird Galley* at the mouth of the Sierra Leone River. The three pirate captains celebrated their victory on board the ship for nearly a month before releasing its captain, William Snelgrave, and giving him back the *Bristol Snow* and the remaining cargo left over from the pirates' week-long occupation of the ship.

Due to his disagreements between the captains Davis and La Buse, Cocklyn went pirating on his own on his ship *Mouroon* with 24 guns on May 10, 1719. Records of Cocklyn's piratical career and life after 1719 are unknown.

Pirates were colorful fellows
By Howard Pyle - 1899

Bartholomew "Black Bart" Roberts

Greatest Pirate of all Captured 470 Ships

Born John Roberts, a Welsh pirate and was the most successful pirate of the Golden Age of Piracy, as measured by vessels captured, taking <u>over 470 prizes</u> in his career. He is widely known as Black Bart, but ironically, this name was never used in his lifetime.

Roberts' first Jolly Roger

Bartholomew Roberts was born in 1682 in Little Newcastle, Wales. His name was originally John Roberts. He is thought to have gone to sea when he was 13 in 1695 however there is no record of him until 1718, when he was mate of a Barbados sloop. A year later he was third mate on the slave ship *Princess*, under Captain Abraham Plumb. In early June of 1719 the *Princess* was anchored at Anambah, on the Gold Coast of West Africa, when she was captured by pirates.

The pirates were in two vessels, the *Royal Rover* and the *Royal James*, and were led by Captain Howell Davis, who was also a Welshman. Roberts forced Roberts and several of the *Princess's* crew to join the Howell Davis pirates.

Davis quickly discovered Roberts' abilities as a navigator and took to consulting him. He was also able to confide to Roberts information in Welsh, thereby keeping it hidden from the rest of the crew. Roberts is said to have been reluctant to become a pirate at first, but soon came to see the advantages of this new lifestyle. Quoting from *"A General History of the Robberies and Murders of the most notorious Pyrates* (1724) Roberts is quoted as saying:

> *In an honest service there is thin commons, low wages, and hard labour. In this, plenty and satiety, pleasure and ease, liberty and power; and who would not balance creditor on this side, when all the hazard that is run for it, at worst is only a sour look or two at choking?*
>
> *No, a merry life and a short one shall be my motto.*

131

Rich Man - Poor Man?

It is easy to understand the lure of piracy; in the merchant navy, Roberts' wage was less than £3 per month (roughly $5 US in 2013) and he had no chance of promotion to captaincy.

A few weeks after Roberts was captured, the pirate's ship *Royal James* had to be abandoned because of worm damage. The remaining pirate ship, *Royal Rover,* headed for the island of Príncipe. Davis hoisted the flags of a British man-of-war, and was allowed to enter the harbor. After a few days Davis invited the governor to lunch on board his ship, intending to hold him hostage for a ransom.

As Davis had to send boats to collect the governor, he was invited to call at the fort for a glass of wine first. The Portuguese had by now discovered that their visitors were pirates, and on the way to the fort Davis' party was ambushed and Davis himself shot dead.

A new captain now had to be elected. Roberts was elected captain by the crew only six

Engraving by Benjamin Cole

weeks of his capture. He accepted of the position, saying, that. . . *since he had dipp'd his Hands in Muddy Water, and must be a Pyrate, it was better being a Commander than a common Man.*

His first act as captain was to lead the crew back to Príncipe to avenge the death of Captain Davis. Roberts and his crew sprang onto the island in the darkness of night, killed a large portion of the male population, and stole all items of value that they could carry away. Soon afterwards he captured a Dutch Guinea ship, then two days later a British ship called the *Experiment*.

The combination of bravery and success that marked this adventure cemented most of the crew's loyalty to Roberts. They concluded that he was "pistol proof" and that they had much to gain by staying with him.

Personal Characteristics

Roberts was a typical pirate captain in his love of fine clothing and jewelry, but had some traits unusual in a pirate, notably a preference for drinking tea rather than rum. He is often described as a teetotaler and a Sabbatarian, but there is no proof of this. He certainly disliked drunkenness while at sea, yet it appears that he drank beer.

Ironically, Roberts' final defeat was facilitated by the drunkenness of his crew. The Sabbatarian claim arises from the fact that musicians were not obliged to play on the Sabbath – this may merely have been intended to ensure the musicians a day's rest, as they were otherwise obliged to play whenever the crew demanded.

Spot of tea?

Black Bart was not as cruel to prisoners as some pirates such as Edward Low, but did not treat them as well as did Samuel Bellamy, Howell Davis or Edward England. Roberts sometimes gave cooperative captains and crews of captured ships gifts, such as pieces of jewelry or items of captured cargo.

Brazil and the Caribbean July 1719 – May 1720

Roberts and his crew crossed the Atlantic and watered and boot-topped their ship (the process of cleaning and painting the area between the water lines of a ship when fully loaded and when unloaded with a protecting layer of antifouling paint). They then spent about nine weeks off the Brazilian coast, but saw no ships. They were about to leave for the West Indies when they encountered a fleet of 42 Portuguese ships in the Todos os Santos' Bay, waiting for two men-of-war of 70 guns each to escort them to Lisbon.

Roberts captured one of the vessels, and ordered her master to point out the richest ship in the fleet. He pointed out a ship of

40 guns and a crew of 170, which Roberts and his men boarded and captured. The ship proved to contain 40,000 Portuguese gold moidores (coins) and jewelry including a cross set with diamonds, designed for the King of Portugal.

Moidores coins were minted from 1640 to 1732 and contained 4.93 grams of gold which, in 2013 dollars, are worth $192.00. Forty thousand of them would produce a value of seven million six hundred eighty million dollars ($7,680,000.00). Not a bad day's work.

Black Bart's new flag showed him standing on two skulls

Black Bart Pirated by a Pirate

Black Bart now headed the *Rover* for Devil's Island off the coast of Guiana to spend some of the booty on a bit of well deserved R&R. A few weeks later they rested and ready for more adventure they made way toward the River Surinam, where they captured a sloop. When a brigantine was sighted, Roberts took forty men to pursue it in the sloop, leaving Walter Kennedy in command of the *Rover*. Roberts' sloop became wind-bound for eight days, and when he was finally able to return, Roberts discovered that Kennedy had sailed off with the *Rover* and what remained of the loot. Roberts and his crew renamed their sloop the *Fortune* and swore on a Bible to uphold new articles, now known as a pirate code.

Barbados Population Fights Back

The inhabitants of Barbados equipped two well-armed ships, the *Summerset* and the *Philipa*, to try to put an end to the pirate menace. In February the two ships began their patrol and on the 26th they encountered two pirate sloops.

In late February 1720 Black Bart had been joined by the French pirate Montigny la Palisse and his sloop, the *Sea King*. When the Barbadian ships attacked the French pirate and the *Sea King* quickly fled and escaped significant damage or capture. Black Bart, after sustaining considerable damage to his ship the *Fortune* broke off the engagement and was also able to

escape. Roberts headed for Dominica to repair the sloop, with
twenty of his crew dying of their wounds on the voyage. There
were also two sloops from Martinique out searching for the
pirates, and Roberts swore vengeance against the inhabitants of
Barbados and Martinique. He had a new flag made with a
drawing of himself standing upon 2 skulls, one labelled ABH (A
Barbadian's Head) and the other AMH (A Martiniquian's Head)

Escapes North to New England

The *Fortune* now headed northwards towards New England
stopping at Newfoundland. Upon arrival "Black Bart" Roberts
raided the town of Canso, Nova Scotia, and captured a number
of ships near Cape Breton and on New England's fishing
ground, the Grand Banks. Roberts then raided the harbor of
Ferryland, capturing a dozen vessels. On June 21, 1720 he
attacked the larger harbor of Trepassey, sailing in with black
flags flying.

All the ships in the harbor were abandoned by their panic-
stricken captains and crews, and the pirates seized whatever
they wanted
without any
resistance
being offered.
Roberts had
captured 22
ships, but was
angered by the
cowardice of
the captains
who had fled
leaving their
ships
defenseless.

Ship on fire

Early every morning, when the morning salute was fired, the
local captains were forced to attend Roberts on board his ship.
If any captain dared to be absent, his ship would be set afire
and destroyed in the harbor for everyone to see.

After his exploits in Newfoundland the Governor of New
England commented that

He hated cowardice, and when the crews of 22 ships in Trepassey harbor fled without firing a shot he was angry at

Ship careened for cleaning hull of marine growth

their failure to defend their ships.

One brig from Bristol was taken over by the pirates to replace the sloop *Fortune* and fitted out with 16 guns. When the pirates left in late June, all the other vessels in the harbor were set on fire.

During July, Roberts captured ten French ships and commandeered one of them, fitting her with 26 cannons and changing her name to the *Good Fortune*. With this more powerful ship, the pirates captured many more vessels in the New England waters before again heading south for the West Indies, accompanied by the French pirate Montigny la Palisse's sloop, which had rejoined them.

In September 1720 the *Good Fortune* was careened and repaired at the island of Carriacou before being renamed the *Royal Fortune*, the first of several ships to be given this name by Roberts. In late September the *Royal Fortune* and the *Fortune* headed for the island of St. Christopher's, and entered Basse Terra Road flying black flags and with their drummers and trumpeters playing. They sailed in among the ships in the Road, all of which promptly struck their flags. The next landfall was at the island of St. Bartholomew, where the French governor allowed the pirates to remain for several weeks to carouse and spend some of their ill gotten loot. By October 25 they were at sea again, off St. Lucia, where they captured up to 15 French and English ships in the next three days. Among the captured ships was the *Greyhound*, whose chief mate, James Skyrme, joined the pirates. He would later become captain of Roberts' consort, the *Ranger*.

During this time, Roberts caught the Governor of Martinique, who was sailing aboard a man-of-war. Robert's ship pulled up next to the man-of-war pretending to be a French merchant ship, and offered information on the location of Captain Roberts before suddenly attacking it, spraying the warship with cannon and small arms fire, after which the pirates boarded it and took it over using pistols and cutlasses. The Governor was caught and promptly hanged on the yardarm of the Royal Fortune.

Pirated by a Pirate yet Again

By the spring of 1721, Roberts' piratical activities had almost brought seaborne trade in the West Indies to a standstill. The *Royal Fortune* and the *Good Fortune* therefore set sail for West Africa and more fertile hunting grounds. On April 18 **Thomas Anstis**, the Consort commander of the *Good Fortune*, left Roberts in the night returning to the Caribbean to raid shipping there and long America's east coast. Roberts and his ship The *Royal Fortune* did not give chase rather, continued towards Africa.

By late April, Bartholomew Roberts was at the Cape Verde islands. The *Royal Fortune* was found to be leaky, and so was abandoned and the pirates transferred to the *Sea King*, which they immediately renamed the *Royal Fortune*. The new *Royal Fortune* made landfall off the Guinea coast in early June, near the mouth of the Senegal River. Two French ships, one of 10 guns and one of 16 guns, gave chase, but were captured by Roberts. Both these ships were commandeered. One, the *Comte de Toulouse*, was renamed the *Ranger*, while the other was named the *Little Ranger* and used as a store ship. Thomas Sutton was made captain of the *Ranger* and James Skyrme captain of the *Little Ranger*.

Roberts now headed for Sierra Leone, arriving on 12 June. Here he was told that two Royal Navy ships, HMS *Swallow* and

HMS *Weymouth*, had left at the end of April, planning to return before Christmas. On August 8 he captured two large ships at Point Cestos, now River Cess in Liberia. One of these was the frigate *Onslow*, transporting soldiers bound for Cape Coast (Cabo Corso) Castle.

A number of the soldiers wished to join the pirates and were eventually accepted, but as landlubbers were given only a quarter share. The *Onslow* was converted to become the fourth *Royal Fortune*. In November and December the pirates careened their ships and relaxed at Cape Lopez and the island of Annobon. Sutton was replaced by Skyrme as captain of the

HMS Swallow opens fire

Ranger. They captured several vessels in January 1722 and then sailed into Ouidah harbor with black flags flying. All the eleven ships at anchor there immediately struck their colors.

Death in Battle

On February 5, 1722 HMS *Swallow*, commanded by Captain Chaloner Ogle, came upon the three pirate ships, the *Royal Fortune*, the *Ranger* and the *Little Ranger* careening at Cape Lopez. The *Swallow* veered away to avoid a shoal, making the pirates think that she was a fleeing merchant ship. The pirate's ship *Ranger*, commanded by James Skyrme, departed in pursuit. Once out of earshot of the other pirates, the *Swallow* opened her gun ports and opened fire. Ten pirates were killed and Skyrme had his leg blown off by a cannonball, but he refused to leave the deck. Eventually, the *Ranger* was forced to strike her colors and the surviving crew was captured.

Five days later, February 10, the *Swallow* returned to Cape Lopez and found the *Royal Fortune* still there. On the previous day, Roberts had captured the *Neptune*, and many of his crew

The crew was drunk when HMS Swallow appeared

were drunk and unfit for duty just when he needed them most.

At first, the pirates thought that the approaching ship was their *Ranger* returning, but a deserter from the recently captured *Swallow* recognized her and alerted Roberts while he was breakfasting with Captain Hill, the master of the *Neptune*.

As was his custom before battle, he quickly dressed himself in his finest clothes. Roberts made a gallant figure being dressed in a rich crimson damask waistcoat and breeches, a red feather in his hat, a gold chain round his neck, with a diamond cross hanging to it, a sword in his hand, and two pairs of pistols slung over his shoulders

Escape Plan Fails – Bartholomew "Black Bart" Roberts is Killed

The pirates' plan was to sail past the HMS *Swallow*, which meant exposing themselves to one broadside. Once past, they would have a good chance of escaping. However, the helmsman failed to keep the *Royal Fortune* on the right course, and the HMS *Swallow* was able to deliver a second broadside.

Captain Roberts was killed by a grape-shot, which struck him in the throat blowing off his head. Before his body could be captured by Captain Ogle, Roberts' wish to be buried at sea was fulfilled by his crew, who weighed his body down and threw it overboard after wrapping it in his ship's sail. His body was never found.

The battle continued for another two hours, until the *Royal Fortune*'s mainmast fell and the pirates signaled for quarter. One member of the crew, John Philips, tried to reach the magazine with a lighted match to blow up the ship, but was prevented by two forced men.

The Aftermath

Only three pirates, including Captain Roberts, had been killed in the battle. A total of 272 men had been captured by the Royal Navy. Of these, 75 were black, and these were sold into slavery. The remainder, apart from those who died on the voyage back, were taken to Cape Coast Castle. 54 were condemned to death, of whom 52 were hanged and two reprieved. Another twenty were allowed to sign indentures with the Royal African Company.

Of the captured pirates who gave their place of birth, 42% were from Cornwall, Devon and Somerset and another 19% from London. There were smaller numbers from northern England and from Wales, and another quarter from a variety of countries including Ireland, Scotland, the West Indies, the Netherlands and Greece. After problems with mutinous Irishmen early in his pirate career, Roberts was known to generally avoid recruiting Irishmen, to the extent that captured merchant sailors would sometimes affect an Irish accent to discourage Roberts from forcing them into his pirate crew.

Captain Chaloner Ogle was rewarded with a knighthood, the only British naval officer to be honored specifically for his actions against pirates. He also profited financially, taking gold dust from Roberts' cabin, and eventually became an Admiral.

The End of the Golden Age of Piracy

Roberts' death shocked the pirate world. The local merchants and civilians had thought him invincible, and some considered him a hero. This battle was to prove a turning point in the war against the pirates, and many historians consider the death of Roberts as marking the end of the Golden Age of Piracy.

Ÿ Pirate Bold.

It is not because of his life of adventure daring that I admire this one of my pet heroes; nor is it because of blowing winds nor ocean nor balmy islands which he knew so nor is it because of gold he spent nor treasure hid. He was a man who knew his own and what he wanted ———— Howard Pyle

Protégés of

Edward Teach a/k/a

"Blackbeard"

Stede Bonnet

Black Caesar

Stede Bonnet

Stede Bonnet was referred to as "The Gentleman Pirate." He was well educated and wealthy landowner and before turning to a life of crime. Bonnet was born into a wealthy English family on the island of Barbados, and inherited the family estate after his father's death in 1694.

In 1709, he married Mary Allamby, and because of marital problems, and despite his lack of sailing experience, Bonnet decided to take to the sea and piracy in the summer of 1717.

Stede Bonnet

In *A General History of the Pyrates*, Charles Johnson wrote that Bonnet was driven to piracy by Mary's nagging and "discomforts he found in a married State."

Despite having no knowledge of shipboard life he contracted a local shipyard to build him a sixty-ton sloop, which he equipped with six guns and named the *Revenge*. This was unusual, as most pirates seized their ships by mutiny or boarding, or else converted a privateer vessel to a pirate ship. Bonnet enlisted a crew of more than seventy men.

He relied on his quartermaster and officers for their knowledge of sailing, and as a result, he was not highly respected by his crew. He traveled with his paid crew along the Eastern Seaboard of what is now the United States from Florida to Maine, capturing vessels and burning others.

Bonnet was seriously wounded during an encounter with a Spanish warship. He retreated to New Providence where he met Edward Teach, the infamous pirate Blackbeard. Who would play a large role in the remainder of Bonnet's life.

Disabled by his wounds, Bonnet temporarily ceded command of the *Revenge* to Blackbeard, but remained aboard as a guest of the more experienced pirate captain. Blackbeard and Bonnet weighed anchor and sailed northward to Delaware Bay, where they plundered eleven ships.

Before separating in December 1717, Blackbeard and Bonnet plundered and captured merchant ships along the East Coast. After Bonnet failed to capture the ship *Protestant Caesar*, his crew abandoned him to join Blackbeard aboard the *Queen Anne's Revenge*.

Bonnet's Jolly Roger

Blackbeard then put one of his henchman in command of Bonnet's *Revenge* and removed Bonnet to the *Queen Anne's Revenge* as a "Guest". Bonnet confided in a few loyal crew members that he was ready to give up his criminal life if he could exile himself in Spain or Portugal. Bonnet would not exercise command again until the summer of 1718.

Bonnet accepts a pardon, changes his name and resumes pirating

When he was pardoned by North Carolina governor Charles Eden and received clearance to go privateering against Spanish shipping, Bonnet was tempted to resume his piracy. However, he did not want to lose his pardon, so he adopted the alias "Captain Thomas" and changed his ship's name to *Royal James* and returned to piracy in July 1718.

In August 1718, Bonnet anchored the *Royal James* on an estuary of the Cape Fear River to careen and repair the ship and wait out the coming hurricane season there.

In late August and September, Colonel William Rhett, with the authorization of South Carolina governor Robert Johnson, led a naval expedition against pirates on the river. Rhett and Bonnet's men fought each other for hours, but the outnumbered pirates ultimately surrendered. Rhett arrested the pirates and brought them to Charleston in early October.

Bonnet escaped on October 24, but was recaptured on Sullivan's Island. On November 10, Bonnet was brought to trial and charged with two acts of piracy. Judge Nicholas Trott sentenced Bonnet to death. Bonnet wrote to Governor Johnson to ask for clemency, but Johnson endorsed the judge's decision, and

Walk the plank

Bonnet was hanged in Charleston on December 10, 1718.

Walking the plank

Bonnet is alleged to have been one of the few pirates to make his prisoners walk the plank.

Black Caesar

African Pirate.

For nearly a decade he served as one of Blackbeard's chief lieutenants aboard the *Queen Anne's Revenge*. He was one of the surviving crew members following Blackbeard's death at the hands of Lieutenant Robert Maynard in 1718.

Black Caesar was widely known for his *"huge size, immense strength, and keen intelligence."*

Black Caesar

He began his pirating career after being shipwrecked in a storm. He would lure passing ships which stopped to give assistance by posing as shipwrecked sailors.

He and a companion continued this ploy for a number of years and amassed a sizable amount of treasure which is reported to be buried on Elliott Key. He and the sailor began to quarrel over a young woman they had brought back from one of the ships they looted. Caesar killed his longtime friend in a duel over her and took the woman for his own.

He began attracting sailors to join him in his piratical activities and soon began attacking ships on the open sea. He and his crew were often able to avoid capture by running onto the mangrove islands. Using a metal ring embedded in a rock, they ran a strong rope through the ring, heel the boat over, and hide their boat in the water until the patrol ship or some other danger went away.

It is thought that he and his men buried 26 bars of silver on the island, although no treasure has ever been recovered.

Had a Large Harem

He grew a harem on his island of least 100 women seized from passing ships. He also had a prison camp in which he held prisoners for ransom. When leaving the island to go on raids, he left no provisions for these prisoners and many eventually starved to death. A few children reportedly escaped captivity, subsisting on berries and shellfish, and formed their own language and customs. This society of lost children give rise to native superstition that the island is haunted.

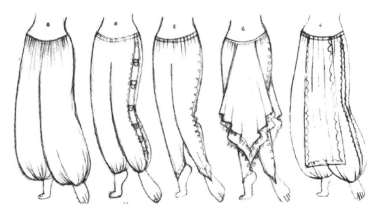

During the early 18th century, Caesar left Biscayne Bay to join Blackbeard in raiding American shipping in the Mid-Atlantic serving as a lieutenant on his flagship *Queen Anne's Revenge*.

In 1718, after Blackbeard's death battling with Lieutenant Robert Maynard at Ocracoke Island, he attempted to set off the powder magazine as per Blackbeard's instructions. However, Caesar was stopped by one of the captives as he prepared to light a trail of gunpowder leading to the magazine. He struggled with the man below decks until several of Maynard's sailors were able to restrain him. Taken prisoner by Virginian colonial authorities, he was convicted of piracy and hanged in Williamsburg, Virginia.

Protégés of
Bartholomew
"Black Bart"
Roberts

Thomas Arstis

Walter Kennedy

Christopher Moody

Thomas Arstis

Arstis served under Captain Howell Davis and Captain Bartholomew Roberts, before setting up on his own account, raiding shipping on the eastern coast of the American colonies.

Captain Thomas Arstis

Anstis is first recorded as a member of the sloop *Buck*, which sailed from Providence, Rhode Island in 1718. During the course of the voyage, Anstis conspired with six other crew members to attempt a mutiny aboard the ship which, upon doing so, stated their intentions to sail southward as pirates.

Howell Davis was elected captain. After Davis' death Bartholomew Roberts replaced him as captain, and eventually had several ships. Anstis was made Consort Captain of one of them, the brigantine *Good Fortune*.

During the night of April 18, 1721, Roberts' ships headed for Africa, but Anstis and his crew in the *Good Fortune* slipped away in the night and continued to operate in the Caribbean. Between Hispaniola and Jamaica, the *Good Fortune* plundered two vessels. Aboard one, the *Irwin*, Anstis's crew committed gang rape and murder against a female passenger. Afterwards they stopped to careen their vessel.

Continuing onward towards Bermuda, Anstis spotted the treasure ship *Morning Star* out from Guinea heading towards the Carolinas. After its capture, the ship was outfitted with 32 guns and placed in the command of ship's gunner John Fenn, Anstis opting to retain command of the smaller *Good Fortune* because of her superior handling.

The two ships continued to sail along the southeastern coast of the colonies until fighting began to break out among many of the forced crew members, and they decided to petition George I of Great Britain for a pardon, claiming they had been forced into piracy by Anstis and Roberts.

Sailing to an island off Cabo San Antonio in Cuba, the crew awaited a reply from the British government for nine months until August 1722, when they received news from their courier ship that their pleas had been ignored, and the king had sent Admiral Sir John Flowers to eradicate the pirates.

On their southward course they encountered the Grand Caymans, where the *Morning Star* ran aground and, as the survivors were being rescued by the *Good Fortune*, the pirates were sighted and pursued by HMS *Hector* and HMS *Adventure*. Anstis was forced to cut his anchor cable and run, finally making his escape under oars when the fresh wind subsided. Anstis lost more than forty of his men on Grand Cayman, most

of these being captured by a landing party from the two Royal Navy vessels, under the command of Flowers.

Anstis and Fenn (who had been rescued from Grand Cayman before the interference of the Royal Navy) now sailed to the Bay of Honduras and careened on an offshore island, capturing three or four prizes en route and augmenting their depleted crew from their captives. Anstis next sailed for the Bahama Islands in early December 1722. On the way, he captured a sloop named *Antelope*, which he added to his squadron, and then a 24-gun ship, which was entrusted to Fenn.

Final days

The pirates put in at Tobago in April, 1723, intending to careen their new vessels, and having just started the task, they were surprised by the British man-of-war Admiral Sir John Flowers' HMS *Winchelsea*. Antis and his men were forced to burn the ship and the sloop and flee into the island's interior, but the *Winchelsea*'s marines overtook and captured them.

British Man Of War

Anstis escaped again in his swift brigantine *Good Fortune*, but his crew, discouraged by their losses, murdered him as he slept in his hammock, and took prisoner all who remained loyal. The mutineers then surrendered to Dutch authorities in Curacao where they received amnesty and their prisoners were hanged.

Walter Kennedy

Kennedy was an English pirate who served as a crew member under pirates Howell Davis and Bartholomew "Black Bart" Roberts.

Kennedy served in the Royal Navy during the War of Spanish Succession, where he heard tales of pirates and dreamed of one day becoming a pirate himself. He was a crew member on the sloop-of-war *Buck*, part of the fleet that Woodes Rogers took to the Bahamas in 1718 to suppress piracy there.

Kennedy's Jolly Roger

Woodes sent the *Buck* to Havana with a letter for the Spanish governor assuring that official that he was not a pirate, but was in Nassau to suppress piracy. Some recently pardoned pirates were added to the crew of the *Buck*, and before it reached Havana they, along with some of the original crew, including Kennedy, mutinied, killing the captain, Jonathan Bass, and other crew members who did not join the mutiny. Howell Davis, another mutineer, was elected captain.

Kennedy was with Davis on the island of Principe when his party was ambushed by the Portuguese. He was the only member of the shore party to escape back to the ship alive.

With Davis dead, Bartholomew Roberts was elected as his successor. When Roberts and forty of the crew chased a possible prize in a captured sloop off the coast of Surinam, Kennedy was left in charge of Roberts' ship, the *Royal Rover*, and a large part of its crew. He took advantage of this to abandon Roberts and proclaim himself captain.

Kennedy headed for Ireland, but having no skill in navigation landed on the north-west coast of Scotland instead. Seventeen of the crew were arrested near Edinburgh and put on trial for piracy, with nine of them being hanged. Kennedy himself was able to reach London where he is said to have kept a brothel in the Deptford Road.

When one of his prostitutes accused him of theft, he was sent to the Bridewell Prison, where he was denounced as a pirate by the mate of a ship he had taken. Kennedy was transferred to the Marshalsea prison and put on trial for piracy. He was hanged at Execution Dock on July 21, 1721 at high noon.

Pirate Walter Kennedy on the Gallows

Christopher Moody

Moody was famous for his cruel policy of "holding no quarter." He had been a member of Black Bart's crew and as such familiar with the waters of Cape Cod. Although he is known primarily for his pirating off the coast of North and South Carolina, he was undoubtedly active in New England as well.

Moody is often remembered for his distinct Jolly Roger flag. Instead of the traditional white on black, Moody's Jolly Roger is gold on red. It also has an hourglass with wings, to express to his victims that their time to live was flying away. In the middle is a white arm holding a dagger. In addition, blood-red pennants were often tied to the ship's mainmast to show deadly intent.

Christopher Moody's distinctive Jolly Roger

He was captured and hanged at Cape Coast Castle in Cabo Corso, Ghana (now Cape Coast, Ghana).

Pirates attack onboard a ship
By Howard Pyle - 1901

Protégé of
Thomas Arstis

John Phillips

John Phillips

Phillips was an English pirate captain. He started his piratical career in 1721 under Thomas Arstis, and stole his own pirate vessel in 1723. He died in a surprise attack by his own prisoners. He is noted for the articles of his ship, the *Revenge,* one of only four complete sets of pirate articles to survive from the Golden Age of Piracy.

The Beginning

John PHILLIPS

Phillips was a ship's carpenter by trade. While voyaging from England to Newfoundland, his ship was captured on April 19, 1721 by Thomas Arstis's pirates. Phillips was forced to join the pirates, as skilled artisans often were. Phillips "was soon reconciled to the life of a Pirate," and served Arstis as carpenter for a year.

In April, 1722, Arstis sent Phillips and some other men ashore on Tobago to repair a captured frigate. A British warship soon arrived, forcing Arstis to flee and abandon Phillips and his comrades. Phillips avoided capture by hiding in the woods, and later returned to Bristol in England with other abandoned shipmates, where they gave up piracy for a time.

A Second Beginning

Some of Phillips' pirate comrades were arrested and imprisoned shortly after their arrival in Bristol, prompting Phillips to take ship again for Newfoundland. There, he conspired to steal a ship and return to piracy. On August 29, 1723, with only four companions, Phillips seized a schooner sailing from Petty Harbor, Newfoundland and renamed her *Revenge,* and embarked on a new piratical career. Phillips' crewmen were John Nutt (sailing master), James Sparks (gunner), Thomas

Fern (carpenter), and William White (tailor and private crewman). They agreed promptly to a set of Articles.

Significantly, Phillips' articles forbade rape under penalty of death; Arstis's crew had committed a notorious gang rape and murder while Phillips was serving with them.

Phillips set sail for the West Indies, capturing several fishing vessels on the way. Aboard one of these captured vessels was John Rose Archer. His addition increased the *Revenge's* total crew to 11. Proceeding to the Caribbean, Phillips and his men hunted for merchantmen near Barbados. They made no captures for three months, and ran severely short of food and supplies, before finally taking some French and English vessels.

Off to the West Indies

They went on to Tobago, where Phillips searched for some of his abandoned comrades from Arstis's crew, but found only one survivor, a black man named Pedro and took Pedro aboard.

Trouble Within the Ranks

The *Revenge* captured a second vessel after leaving Tobago and made the carpenter Thomas Fern consort captain in charge of the prize. Fern and the crew, attempted to escape with the stolen vessel. The *Revenge* overtook Fern and captured him, killing one of the prize crew and wounding another. Fern and one of his crewmates tried and failed to escape again later that winter, and Phillips killed them both.

The killing has been described as being "pursuant to their Articles," but as Phillips' Article II specifies marooning rather than outright execution as the punishment for running away, this may be an error or may reflect the articles being amended at some point.

Somewhere to the north of Tobago, in March 1723, Phillips captured two more ships, killing a ship's master named Robert Mortimer when the latter attacked the pirates in an attempt to regain his vessel.

Head Back North

The pirates continued northward arriving at Cape Sable, Nova Scotia on April 1, 1723. Here Phillips met great success as he raided New England fishing vessels working the fishing banks between Cape Sable and Sable Island. His men robbed some 13 vessels over the course of a few days. One vessel they spared was a schooner which belonged to William Minott, the original owner of *Revenge* as Phillips declared "We have done him enough injury.

The End

In April, 1724, the sloop *Squirrel* of Annisquam, MA, commanded by Andrew Haraden, while engaged on a fishing voyage was taken by Phillips. The *Squirrel* was a fine new craft, therefore Phillips abandoned his own vessel and appropriated the fisherman for his piratical purposes.

The vessel had been sent to sea so hastily that the craft had not been finished inside, consequently tools were left aboard to complete the work when the conditions were unfavorable for fishing.

Phillips employed Haraden and the other prisoners in the finishing of the craft. One of the men, Edward Cheeseman planned a recapture. Midnight of the 18th was the time appointed.

The vessel was ploughing through the water at a lively rate when Cheeseman seized John Nott, one of the pirate chiefs, who was on deck and threw him overboard. At the same time

160

Haraden despatched Phillips with a blow from an adze, James Sparks the pirates' gunner suffered the same fate as Nott, while a man named Burrell, the boatswain was killed with a broad axe. Capt. Haraden sailed home to Annisquam with the heads of Phillips and Burrell fixed at the mast head of the recaptured craft.

His captors cut off his head and pickled it so they could prove to officials in Boston that they had done in the infamous pirate Captain Phillips.

A number of prisoners were brought in, but on trial at Boston all but two were acquitted on the charge of piracy, it being held that they were forced men. Four, John Rose Archer, William White, William Phillips and William Taylor were found guilty of piracy and were sentenced to death.

The pirates gave widely reprinted speeches before their executions. Archer blamed drinking but also blamed brutal merchant captains who drove oppressed sailors to seek piracy as a tempting way to escape.

They pickled his head

The first two were hung at Charlestown Ferry and White's body was suspended in irons on Bird Island. The last two were reprieved for a year and a day to be recommended to the King's mercy. It is said that Hangman's Island in Annisquam river, now covered by the raiload bed received the name from the fact that two of the bodies of the dead pirates were suspended from gibbets erected in its center.

The General Court granted Haraden, Cheeseman and Philmore £42 each, and £32 each to five others concerned in the recapture and breaking up of this dangerous gang of buccaneers.

Archer was temporarily spared, but died on the gallows at Boston with three of the other pirates on June 2, 1724. Phillips had survived less than eight months as a pirate captain but in this short period he had captured 34 ships.

Important Legacy

Phillips was essentially a small-time criminal as compared to pirates like Roberts; he commanded only a small schooner, and at the time of his death he had just 11 men under his command.

Never the less, Phillips is important to scholars of piracy because his articles have survived, through reprinting in Charles Johnson's *General History of the Pyrates*. Only three other complete or near-complete sets of articles appear in the secondary literature. These few articles underpin much of scholarly insight into life aboard pirate vessels.

The Phillips story is also significant as an example of the short-lived but destructive bands of pirates who branched out from much larger pirate crews led by Arstis and Blackbeard.

Phillips' captor and mentor, Arstis, had himself been captured by Bartholomew Roberts, who was in turn a former captive of Howell Davis, who had turned to piracy after falling into Edward England's hands. This line sprang originally from the pirate den at New Providence which had served as a base for Davis, England, and many other robber captains.

Captain John Phillips's Articles

I. Every Man Shall obey civil Command; the Captain shall have one full Share and a half of all Prizes; the Master, Carpenter, Boatswain and Gunner shall have one Share and quarter.

II. If any Man shall offer to run away, or keep any Secret from the Company, he shall be marooned with one Bottle of Powder, one Bottle of Water, one small Arm, and Shot.

III. If any Man shall steal any Thing in the Company, or game, to the Value of a Piece of Eight, he shall be marooned or shot.

IV. If any time we shall meet another Marooner that Man shall sign his Articles without the Consent of our Company, shall suffer such Punishment as the Captain and Company shall think fit.

V. That Man that shall strike another whilst these Articles are in force, shall receive Moses' Law (that is, 40 Stripes lacking one) on the bare Back.

VI. That Man that shall snap his Arms, or smoke Tobacco in the Hold, without a Cap to his Pipe, or carry a Candle lighted without a Lanthon shall suffer the same Punishment as in the former Article.

VII. That Man shall not keep his Arms clean, fit for an Engagement, or neglect his Business, shall be cut off from his Share, and suffer such other Punishment as the Captain and the Company shall think fit.

VIII. If any Man shall lose a Joint in time of an Engagement, shall have 400 Pieces of Eight ; if a Limb, 800.

IX. If at any time you meet with a prudent Woman, that Man that offers to meddle with her, without her Consent, shall suffer present Death.

Phillips' Jolly Roger

Phillips' flag was turned over to Massachusetts authorities when his victorious prisoners sailed the *Revenge* into Annisquam. The Boston News-Letter described the flag as follows: "their own dark flag, in the middle of which an anatomy, and at one side of it a dart in the heart, with drops of blood proceeding from it; and on the other side an hour-glass.

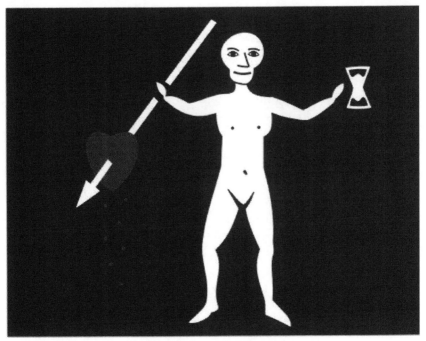

John Phillip's Jolly Roger

164

Protégé of
John Phillips

John Rose Archer

John Rose Archer

John Rose Archer was a Newfoundland fisherman. His boat was captured by the pirate John Phillips and he was taken prisoner. He took readily to a pirate's life and soon was elected quartermaster by the pirate crew.

Pressed a US President's Great, Great Grandfather into Service

On September 5, 1723 they attacked the sloop *Dolphin*. Aboard was John Fillmore, great-grandfather of the later U.S. president Millard Fillmore, and he was forced into service as a pirate.

Rose left Captain Phillips to join up with Blackbeard and little is known of him save his trial, conviction and hanging on June 2, 1724 in Boston for his crimes as a pirate.

Written accounts by John Fillmore of life aboard Phillips' schooner *Revenge* is one of the few surviving primary sources by an eyewitness to piracy during the Golden Age.

Pirate's hanging

Protégé of
Henry Jennings

Charles Vane

Charles Vane

Charles Vane was an English pirate operating out of the pirate's base at New Providence in the Bahamas who preyed upon English and French shipping. His pirate career lasted a relatively long time for pirates, from 1715 to 1721. His flagship was a brigantine named the *Ranger*.

Charles Vane arrived in Port Royal sometime during the War of the Spanish Succession. In 1715, he began serving under the infamous pirate Henry Jennings.

In late July of 1715, a Spanish treasure fleet was hit by a hurricane off the coast of Florida, dumping tons of Spanish gold and silver not far from shore. As the surviving Spanish sailors salvaged what they could, pirates made a beeline for the wreck site.

Jennings (with Vane on board) was the first to reach the site, and his buccaneers raided the Spanish camp on shore, making off with some £87,000 in recovered gold and silver.

The King's Pardon: In 1718, the King of England issued a blanket pardon for all pirates who wished to return to an honest life. Many accepted, including Jennings. Vane, however, scoffed at the

Early 18th Century Engraving of Charles Vane

notion of retirement from piracy and soon became the leader of those who refused the pardon.

Vane and a handful of other pirates outfitted a small sloop, the *Lark*, for service as a pirate vessel. On February 23, 1718, the royal frigate HMS *Phoenix* arrived in Nassau. Vane and his men were captured, but were released as a goodwill gesture. Within a couple of weeks, Vane and some of his die-hard companions were ready to once again take to piracy. Soon he had forty of Nassau's worst cutthroats, including seasoned buccaneer Edward England and "Calico Jack" Rackham, who would himself become a notorious pirate captain.

Vane's Reign of Terror: Vane was infamous for his cruelty toward the crews of captured vessels. After his first act as a pirate he was reported to the governor of Bermuda for torturing men on rival vessels while on a salvage mission. He also showed scant respect for the pirate code, cheating his own crews out of their fair share of plunder and killing surrendered sailors after promising them mercy. By April of 1718, Vane had a handful of small ships and was ready for action. In that month, he captured twelve merchant ships.

Vane and his men treated the sailors and merchants cruelly in spite of the fact that they had surrendered instead of fought. One sailor was bound hand and foot and tied to the top of the bowsprit and the pirates threatened to shoot him if he did not tell where the treasure on board was located. Fear of Vane drove commerce in the area to a halt.

The torture begins

Charles Vane takes Nassau: Vane subsequently traded up ships by capturing first a Barbados sloop and then a large 12-gun brigantine, each of which he named the *Ranger* in turn. His brutal attacks became well known. Captain Vane was cornered in February 1718 by Vincent Pearse, commander of the HMS *Phoenix*.

Word had recently spread of the Royal Pardon offered to pirates in exchange for a guarantee they would quit plundering, so Vane claimed he'd actually been en route to surrender to Pearse and accepted the pardon on the spot, gaining his freedom though losing his captured ship, the *Lark*.

As soon as he was free of Pearse he ignored the pardon and resumed his depredations. Vane knew that Woodes Rogers, the new governor, would be arriving soon. Vane decided that his position in Nassau was too weak, so he set out to capture a proper pirate ship.

He soon took a 20-gun French ship and made it his flagship. In June and July of 1718, he seized many more small merchant vessels, more than enough to keep his men happy. Vane triumphantly re-entered Nassau, essentially taking over the town. Vane controlled the Nassau harbor and the small fort, which flew a pirate flag from its flagpole.

Vane's bold escape: In August 1718, the new Governor of New Providence, Woodes Rogers, and two men-of-war arrived in Nassau to oversee the pardon, and more importantly for Vane, capture those who violated it.

While most pirates accepted the enforced pardon, Vane resisted it and any who attempted to honestly reform. He made an impression by firing on the Royal Navy immediately, and sent a letter to Rogers demanding to be allowed to dispose of his

Captures larger ship

plundered goods before accepting the King's pardon. As night fell, Vane knew his situation was impossible, so he set fire to his flagship and sent it towards the Navy ships, hoping to destroy them by fire.

The Navy ships were able to hurriedly cut their anchor lines to get away, but Vane and his men escaped in his fast six-gun sloop, the *Ranger*, defiantly firing at the governor as he passed and threatening to return. He evaded the few Royal Navy vessels in the area and sailed north.

Charles Vane and Blackbeard

"Fire Ship" sails toward naval ship

Vane continued practicing piracy on the open seas, amassing a large crew and three ships. He was so successful, in fact, that Governor Rogers sent out Colonel William Rhett to hunt Vane down.

Meanwhile, Vane had given command of one of his ships to a fellow pirate by the name of Yeats and, looking to emulate Blackbeard's success,the two pillaged and looted vessels that were entering and leaving the port at Charleston,.

However, Vane created division among his crew by refusing to capture several promising vessels, leading Yeats to abscond in the night with a large portion of treasure and one of the captured brigs. Vane continued pirating with some success.

He headed to North Carolina where Edward "Blackbeard" Teach had gone semi-legitimate. The two pirate crews socialized for a week in October 1718 on the shores of Ocracoke Island. Vane hoped to convince his old friend to join him in an attack on Nassau, but Blackbeard declined, having too much to lose.

Vane then turned north toward New England. On November 23, Vane ordered an attack on a frigate which turned out to be a French Navy warship. Out-gunned, Vane broke off the fight and fled.

His men, led by the reckless crewman Calico Jack Rackham, had wanted to stay and fight and take the French ship. The next day, the crew deposed Vane as captain, electing Rackham instead. Vane and fifteen others were given a small sloop and the two pirate crews went their separate ways. Sailing south again, Vane set about clawing his way back up the pirate ranks by seizing ever larger ships.

Capture and Execution

Vane's final blow came after his ship was wrecked in a storm in February 1719, separating him from his consort, Robert Deal. One of the only survivors, Vane was washed up on an uninhabited island in the Bay of Honduras.

Eventually a ship arrived, but unfortunately for Vane it was commanded by an old acquaintance and former buccaneer Captain Holford. Holford would not rescue Vane from the island stating:

> *"Charles, I shan't trust you aboard my ship, unless I carry you a prisoner; for I shall have you plotting with my men, knock me on the head and run away with my ship a pirating."*

Before departing, Holford stated that he would be back on the island in a month, and threatened that if he found Vane still there, he would take him back to Jamaica and hang him.

Another ship soon arrived and as none of the crew recognized Vane he was allowed on board. Unluckily, Captain Holford's ship met with this ship at sea, and the captain of Vane's ship invited Holford, a friend of his, to dine with him.

While there, Holford saw Vane working aboard and informed the captain just who Vane truly was. The captain quickly arrested Vane and turned him over to Captain Holford who locked him in his hold. Upon arriving in Jamaica Vane was promptly turned over to the authorities.

His reputation had earned the disdain of pirates, royal mariners and the public at large and they all wanted him to rot in jail before being executed. It is reported he remained in jail for more than a year before he was finally hung.

During his trial, he was found guilty and sentenced to death on March 22, 1720. At his trial, numerous witnesses from merchant vessels captured by Vane testified against him, as did Vincent Pearse, Captain of the HMS *Phoenix*, who related how Vane had made a mockery of the King's pardon. When it was Vane's turn to present his defense, he called no witnesses and

On the gallows

asked no questions. On March 29, 1721, Vane was hanged at Gallows Point in Port Royal.

He died without the least remorse for his crimes. After death, his body was hung from a gibbet on Gun Cay, at the mouth of harbor at Port Royal, as a warning to others against piracy.

Captain Kidd buries treasure at Gardiner's Island
By Howard Pyle - 1898

Protégé of
Charles Vane

"Calico Jack" Rackham

Jack "Calico Jack" Rackham

He was only active for a few years in the Caribbean, but he ended up shaping some of the motifs we've come to recognize as part of pirate lore.

The Jolly Roger, the black flag featuring the skull and crossbones, was his idea, though earlier versions featured two cutlasses instead of crossbones.

The Original Jolly Roger

He had a penchant for wearing clothes made from bright Indian Calico cloth, which lead his fellow pirates to dub him "Calico Jack". At the time of Woodes Rogers' arrival in New Providence Rackhan was serving in the crew of Charles Vane, leader of the die-hard pirate faction.

By November, 1718, Rackham was serving as Vane's quartermaster aboard an unnamed brigantine. On the 23rd of that month, Vane was voted out of power by his crew for refusing to engage a French man-of-war in the approaches to the Windward Passage. Calico Jack was chosen as his replacement and Vane and fifteen of his loyalists left the ship's company in a small boat.

Rackham's command was not particularly successful, showing courage, but a lack of judgment. He chose to cruise around Jamaica, the center of British power in the Caribbean and the headquarters of the Royal Navy's West Indies squadron.

In December he captured a richly-laden merchant ship (the *Kingston*) within sight of Port Royal, provoking the merchants there to outfit several privateers to apprehend him.

Three months later, they found Rackham south of Cuba, still in his brigantine with the *Kingston* anchored alongside. Rackham and most of his crew were dozing ashore in a camp of tents made from old sails, and hid in the woods while their ships were captured.

Left without vessels, Rackham and six followers sailed around Cuba to Nassau in a small boat, a trip that took them nearly three months. Claiming they had been forced into piracy by Vane, they convinced Governor Rogers to pardon them.

Rackham settled in Nassau, where he entered into a passionate

Becalmed pirates row their skiff

affair with Anne Bonny, the fiery young wife of John Bonny, a pirate who had turned informer. In mid 1720, the lovers approached John (the husband) and convinced him to annul their marriage in exchange for a cash payment.

Unfortunately, Governor Rogers refused to countenance the arrangement. Unable to continue their relationship ashore, Rackham and Bonny decided to return to piracy. The couple recruited a half-dozen ex-pirates, stole a swift sloop, and snuck out of Nassau on the night of August 22, 1720.

Later, privateers would catch up with him and take Rackham and his remaining crew into custody. He was found guilty and hung at Gallows Point in Port Royal on November 18, 1720. His body was later placed in a gibbet on a small sandbar in the harbor now known as Rackham's Cay

Captain Kidd on the deck of the Adventure Galley
By Howard Pyle - 1899

Protégés of

"Calico Jack" Rackham

Mary Read
Anne Bonny

Mary Read

She and Anne Bonny are two of the most famed female pirates of all time; they are the only two women known to have been convicted of piracy during the Golden Age of Piracy.

Mary Read was born in England as the illegitimate child of a widowed sea captain's wife.

Read's widowed mother began to disguise illegitimately born Mary as a boy after the death of Mary's older, legitimate brother Mark.

This was done in order to continue to receive financial support from his paternal grandmother. The grandmother was

Pirate Mary Read

apparently fooled, and Read and her mother lived on the inheritance into her teenage years. Still dressed as a boy, Read then found work as a footboy, and later found employment on a ship.

She subsequently joined the British military who were allied with Dutch forces against the French during the War of the Spanish Succession. Read, in male disguise, proved herself through battle, but she fell in love with a Flemish soldier. When they married, she used their military commission and gifts from intrigued brethren in arms as a funding source to acquire an inn named "De drie hoefijzers" (The Three Horseshoes") near Breda Castle in The Netherlands.

Upon her husband's premature death, Read again resumed male dress and military service in Holland. With peace, there was no room for advancement in the military, so she quit and boarded a ship bound for the West Indies. Read's ship was

taken by pirates, who forced her to join them. Later she took
the King's pardon c.1718-1719, and took a commission to
privateer, until that ended with her joining the crew in mutiny.

In 1720 she joined pirate John "Calico Jack" Rackham and his
companion, the female pirate Anne Bonny. Read remained
dressed as a man at first. Nobody knew that Read was female
until Bonny began to take a liking to Read thinking she was a
handsome young fellow.

That forced Read to reveal to Bonny that she was a woman.
Rackham, who was Bonny's lover, became jealous of the
friendship between them and threatened to cut the throat of
Bonny's new friend.

To prevent Read's death, Rackham was also let in on the secret.
Rackham decided to break male seafaring tradition by allowing
both women to remain on the crew. During their brief cruise in
late 1720, they took several prisoners and forced them into
useful service. Mary fell in love with one such victim who was

Mary fighting on deck

surprised to learn that she was a woman and he eventually
returned the affection.

In October 1720, pirate hunter Captain Jonathan Barnet took
Rackham's crew by surprise while they were hosting a rum
party with another crew of Englishmen off the west coast of

Jamaica. After a volley of fire left the pirate vessel disabled, Rackham's crew and their "guests" fled to the ship's hold, leaving only the women and one other to fight Barnet's boarding party.

Allegedly, Read angrily shot into the hold, killing one, wounding others when the men would not come up and fight with them. Barnet's crew eventually overcame the women. Rackham surrendered, requesting "quarter."

Rackham and his crew were arrested and brought to trial in what is now known as Spanish Town, Jamaica, where they were sentenced to hang for acts of piracy, as were Read and Bonny.

However, the women escaped the noose when they revealed they were both "quick with child" (known as "Pleading the belly"), so they received a temporary stay of execution. Read died in prison in April 1721, but there is no record of burial of her baby.

Anne Bonny

Little is known of Bonny's life, particularly prior to her beginning her career as a pirate. It is believed that she was born in Ireland in 1702. Information dealing with her life is scarce and most modern knowledge stems from Charles Johnson's *A General History of the Pyrates.*

Bonny's family travelled to the new world very early on in her life; at first the family had a rough start in their new home. Her mother died shortly after they arrived in North America.

Pirate Anne Bonny

Her father attempted to establish himself as an attorney, but did not do well. Eventually, Bonny's father joined the more profitable merchant business and accumulated a substantial fortune. It is recorded she had red hair and was considered a "good catch", but may have had a fiery temper; at aged 13 she supposedly stabbed a servant girl with a table knife.

She married a poor sailor and small-time pirate named James Bonny. James Bonny hoped to win possession of his father-in-law's estate, but Anne was disowned by her father.

Between 1714 and 1718, she and James Bonny moved to New Providence; known as a sanctuary for pirates. It is also recorded that after the arrival of Governor Woodes Rogers in the summer of 1718, James Bonny became an informant for the governor.

Rackham's mistress

While in the Bahamas, Bonny began mingling with pirates in the local taverns. She met Jack "Calico Jack" Rackham, captain of the pirate sloop *Revenge*, and became his mistress. They had a child in Cuba, who eventually took the name of Cunningham. Many different theories state that he was left with his family or simply abandoned.

Bonny rejoined Rackham and continued the pirate life, having left her husband and marrying Rackham while at sea. Bonny and Rackham escaped to live together as pirates. Bonny, Rackham, and Mary Read stole the *Revenge*, then at anchor in Nassau harbor, and put out to sea.

Anne was a fierce fighter

Rackham and the two women recruited a new crew. Over the next several months, they were successful as pirates, capturing many ships and bringing in an abundance of treasure.

Bonny did not disguise herself as a man aboard the *Revenge* as is often claimed. She took part in combat alongside the men, and the accounts of her exploits present her as competent, effective in combat, and respected by her shipmates.

Mary Read's name and gender were known to all from the start. Governor Rogers had named them in a "Wanted Pirates" circular published in the continent's only newspaper, *The Boston News-Letter*. Although Bonny has historical renown as a female Caribbean pirate, she never commanded a ship of her own.

Capture and imprisonment

In October 1720, Rackham and his crew were attacked by a "King's ship", a sloop captained by Jonathan Barnet under a commission from the Governor of Jamaica. Most of Rackham's pirates did not put up much resistance as many of them were too drunk to fight; other sources indicate it was at night and most of them were asleep. However, Read, Bonny, and an unknown man fought fiercely and managed to hold off Barnet's troops for a short time.

Rackham and his crew were taken to Jamaica, where they were convicted and sentenced by the Governor of Jamaica to be hanged. According to Johnson, Bonny's last words to the imprisoned Rackham were that she was "sorry to see him there, but if he had fought like a Man, he need not have been hang'd like a Dog."

After being sentenced, Read and Bonny both "pleaded their bellies": asking for mercy because they were pregnant.

In accordance with English common law, both women received a temporary stay of execution until they gave birth. Read died in prison, most likely from a fever, though it has been alleged that she died during childbirth.

Disappearance

There is no historical record of Bonny's release or of her execution. This has fed speculation that her father ransomed her; that she might have returned to her husband, or even that she resumed a life of piracy under a new identity.

The *Oxford Dictionary of National Biography* states that "Evidence provided by the descendants of Anne Bonny suggests that her father managed to secure her release from jail and bring her back to Charles Town, South Carolina,

Mother of ten more children

On December 21, 1721 she married a local man, Joseph Burleigh, and they had 10 children. She died in South Carolina, a respectable woman, at the age of eighty on April 22, 1782. She was buried on April 24, 1782. According to Sherman Carmichael's *Forgotten Tales of South Carolina*, she is buried in the York County Churchyard in York County, Virginia.

Some claim that she was smuggled away by her father, and that this was made possible by his far reaching and favorable merchant connections. This is a probable solution to the mystery. After all, her father's business connections had saved Anne a number of times before. Rackham's crew spent a lot of time in Jamaica and the surrounding area. Although the crew, including Anne, was discovered or caught on a number of occasions, Bonny always escaped punishment and harm. It is surmised that this was probably because of her father's business contacts in Jamaica.

Protégé of

Samuel

"Black Sam"

Bellamy's

Henry Jennings

Henry Jennings

Jennings was a British privateer who was active during the War of Spanish Succession and later served as leader and unofficial mayor of the pirate haven of New Providence.

Although little is known of Jennings' early life, he was first recorded as a privateer during the War of the Spanish Succession operating from Jamaica which was then governed by Lord Archibald Hamilton. There is evidence that Jennings owned enough land in Jamaica to live comfortably, thus leaving

Ruthless Henry Jennings

his motivations for piracy to conjecture.

His first recorded act of piracy took place in early 1716 when, with three vessels and 300 men, Jennings' fleet ambushed the Spanish salvage camp from the 1715 Treasure Fleet. After forcing the retreat of around 60 soldiers, Jennings set sail for Jamaica carrying back an estimated 350,000 pesos.

While en route to Jamaica, Jennings encountered another Spanish ship and captured another 60,000 pesos.

When Jennings encountered "Black Sam" Bellamy of the Whydah fame, he teamed with him to commit more piracies against the French. When Bellamy double-crossed him, Jennings' ruthlessness was evidenced in the brutal slaying of more than 20 Frenchmen and Englishmen, and the burning of an innocent Englishman's merchant sloop.

Jennings was declared a pirate by the very governor who had commissioned him & originally condoned his actions (taking a cut for himself). Jennings was forced to flee from Jamaica and eventually established a new base of operations in New Providence in the Bahamas.

Based out of Nassau for a time, Jennings became an unofficial mayor of the growing pirate colony and retires from piracy.

In early 1718, Jennings surrendered to authorities following the general amnesty declared by the newly appointed Governor of

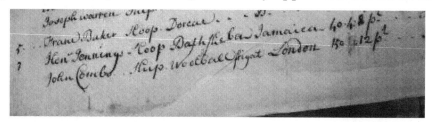

Henry Jennings' ship Bathsheba clears customs at Boston in the summer of 1715, just prior to his descent into piracy.
From Massachusetts customs records

the Bahamas, Woodes Rogers. He retired as a wealthy plantation owner in Bermuda, where he received his pardon.

He is one of very few pirates said to have enjoyed a successful retirement. It is unknown what his ultimate fate was, though some historians speculate that he was captured by the Spanish in his later years, dying in ambiguity in a New Spain prison. Other legends have him growing old with his family in Bermuda.

Pirates fighting on the beach
By Howard Pyle - 1899

Non "Flying Gang" Pirates Active in New England Waters

Thomas Tew's "Jolly Roger"

Joe Bradish (Brodish)

Buried Treasure on Block Island?
Hung alongside Capt Kidd!

In the fall of 1698 he was aboard the *Adventurer* anchored off the island of Polonais on their way to Borneo. While most of the officers and passengers were ashore Brandish raised anchor and sailed away. Below deck the crew found nine chests filled to the brim with Spanish Treasure. They then sailed to Long Island where many of the crew debarked, bought farms and livestock to live the remainder of their days as respectable citizen.

Brandish then sailed the *Adventurer* to Block Island and, fearing interception by government ships prowling the waters in search of pirates, landed and off-loaded many bags containing pieces of eight, silver and jewels. They then shot a cannon ball through the ship's bottom sending her to a watery grave, boarded one of their captured merchant ships

Pirates burying treasure

and, sailed for Boston. Some speculate the treasure is still buried on Block Island waiting to be found.

Many locations on the island have been rumored to be the hiding place of pirate's plunder and treasure. Mohegan Bluff, Sandy Point and the beach at Southwest Point are three locations where pieces of eight and other coins reportedly have been found over the years.

Captain Brandish then sailed to Boston where he was captured and jailed. He was allowed to escape by jailer Caleb Ray, a relative of Brandish. He was recaptured, placed in irons and, with notorious Captain Kidd, shipped off to England aboard the man-of-war *Advice* to be tried and executed for acts of piracy.

Pirate Captain Jack Quelch

Isle of Shoals Treasure

In July, 1703, John Quelch was a lieutenant on the *Charles,* a ship based in Marblehead, Massachusetts. The *Charles's* crew mutinied and locked its ailing Captain Plowman in his cabin. The crew elected Quelch the captain and Plowman was thrown overboard

Under Quench's command the crew plundered nine Portuguese ships off the coast of Brazil. The total value is estimated at over 4 million in today's money.

Quelch was captured north of Cape Cod while hiding gold nuggets on Isle of Shoals' Smuttynose Island. Also, before being captured, legend says the crew had buried some of the gold on Star Island across from Smuttynose Island. In the 1800s some gold coins were found hidden in a stone wall there. No one has reported finding more coins. Does that mean no more has been found and that all the gold is gone?

Old Roger

Popular myth has it that John Quelch flew a pirate flag referred to as Old Roger by his crew. It is sometimes considered to be the origin of the name Jolly Roger. It is also alleged that his theme was later borrowed by Blackbeard as well as Bartholomew "Black Bart" Roberts.

"Old Roger"

There is no evidence whatsoever that Quelch flew any flag other than the Flag of St. George or possibly a privateer's flag of St. George quartered on a red background similar to today's British merchant colors. Courtroom testimony from the crew maintained that the flag of England had been flown at all times.

Pirate Thomas Pound

Pardoned in the nick of time

Thomas was a "stay at home" pirate in that he pirated exclusively in northeast waters. Thomas Pound always wanted to be a pirate. However, he lacked both a ship and provisions. However, he would not let that stand in the way of his attaining his goal. He set about developing a complicated and circuitous plan.

First, he hired a fisherman, Thomas Hawkins, to sail him along with five others, to Nantasket six miles south of Boston by sea. Outside Boston Harbor, at Long Island, they picked up five heavily armed men and commandeered Hawkins's small boat. Pound's life as a pirate had begun.

He convinced Hawkins to join their crew and, later that day; they captured the ketch *"Mary"* just outside Marblehead Harbor, near Halfway Rock. They transferred to this larger ship giving her captain, Allen Char, Hawkins' smaller fishing vessel with which to return to shore. This would prove to be a fatal mistake because, as soon as Char reached shore the *"Mary's"* captain outfitted his ship with cannon and immediately set to sea in pursuit of the fledgling pirates.

Apparently, one fisherman, John Darby, decided to abandoned his wife and five children, in order join Pound's crew. Next stop was Fort Royal in Casco Bay to pick up more crewmembers, soldiers who had agreed to desert and join Pound's pirate crew.

The six deserting soldiers had stolen cannon, guns and ammunition with which to arm their pirate ship. Once all were on board, they set sail to the Elizabeth Islands in Nantucket Sound where they attacked the sloop *Good Speed* and the brigantine *Merrimack* and other Cape Cod shipping.

194

Sailing out of Nantucket Sound, south of Cape Cod, the sloop ran into a stiff northeaster and was forced away to Virginia. Here, Pound managed to fetch some other spoil in the shape of an old sail, a piece of linen cloth and some dyes, before heading back towards Massachusetts. On their way, Hawkins noticed that they were being followed; but they finally outran their pursuer.

Not long after they had reached Cape Cod, Thomas Hawkins, who was getting tired of Pound's maneuvering, succeeded in making his escape. He met Captain Jacobus Loper, a Portuguese whaler, who was getting ready to sail for Boston. Here, Hawkins thought that he would be safe and escape the grip of the law. But instead Loper thought best to turn him over to the Boston authorities and soon Hawkins was shackled and safely lodged in prison.

As soon as the *"Mary"* reached the *"Good Speed"*, Pound, in his surprise, climbed on deck with his sword flourishing in his hand and shouting: "Come you Dogs, and I will strike you presently". When he was told that if he would yield they would be given good quarter, he replied: "Ei yee Dogs, we will give you quarter by and by."

Pirate in Shackles

But it was not long before Pound himself was hit by a bullet, when "several bones were taken out." There were casualties on both sides. The pirates were finally captured and brought to Boston, fourteen of them. Most of them, including Pound and Hawkins, were found guilty of felony, piracy and murder. They were sentenced to be "hanged by the neck until they be dead."

Just in the Nick of Time

Jan. 27, 1690, the day that the hanging was to take place, Hawkins had the rope around his neck already, when someone ran to tell the hangman that the Governor had postponed the hanging. He was completely pardoned, probably at the request of his sisters, who had married high ranking officers of the colony. Finally, all, except one, received their pardon, Pound included. Pound and Hawkins were then placed on the "*Rose*" to be sent into exile in England.

Reaching Cape Sable, the "*Rose*" was intercepted by a French privateer of thirty guns, and a vigorous combat took place. The captain of the "*Rose*" was slain and several others; Hawkins finally died of his wounds. Somewhat bruised, the "*Mary*" was able to reach England, without any other incidents.

Battle at Sea

Here, Thomas Pound was pardoned entirely for whatever mischiefs he would have done on the coast of the American colony. He even wrote right away to Governor Andros of Massachusetts, who was in London, giving him the latest news from New England. In 1691, he published in London "A New Map of New England." It served as a basis for other charts for nearly fifty years after.

On August 5, 1690, just a few months after his arrival in England, he was appointed captain of the frigate "*Sally Rose*", of the Royal Navy. In 1697, his ship was stationed at Virginia under his old patron Governor Andros. In 1699, he retired to private life and died in 1703, at Isleworth, county Middlesex, a "gentleman, respected by friends and neighbors".

Captain Ned (Edward) LOWE

Cruelest pirate upon the seas

Born in London, England in the late 1600s, he was a petty thief and pickpocket before coming to Boston where he became legitimately employed as rigger in one of Boston's many shipyards.

In May 1722 he and group of others set sail for Honduras. The original plan was to steal a shipload of lumber for resale in Boston. Something went wrong and he and his crew were forced off the ship.

The next day Lowe, and his soon to be pirates, stole a sloop and set of in search of ships to plunder. After capturing several ships he chose the 80 ton schooner *The Fancy* as flagship of his pirate fleet.

Lowe was described as a "maniac and a brute" by his own crew. His needless brutality was so severe that authorities made particular efforts to capture him and eventually his crew cast him adrift mid ocean in a small boat without any provisions.

Some examples of his senseless cruel and brutal actions, He;

- Made the commander of a Nantucket whaler slice off his own ears and eat them before he killed him.
- Personally slaughtered fifty-three officers of the Spanish galleon "Montcova", and forced one, before killing him, to eat the heart of a fellow officer.
- Cut off a victim's lips, cooked them, and forced the victim to eat his own lips before he slaughtered him.
- Burned a French cook alive saying he was a "greasy fellow who would fry well"

197

Lowe is said to have enjoyed torturing his captives. Few who were taken as captives aboard Low's ship ever debarked alive.

One of his sadistic torture sessions apparently went wrong and Lowe was cut severely about his mouth. The medical attention he received went wrong and he was left with an ugly scar as his reward.

He was the captain who the real Robinson Crusoe, Marblehead's Philip Ashton, escaped from by hiding on a deserted Caribbean island in June of 1722.

Lowe's end came after he was rescued from the sea, having been set adrift by his own crew, by a passing French ship.

However, when they discovered his true identity, the French mariners gave him a cursory trial and then hung him from the yardarm until he was dead. The year was 1724.

Another version of Low's demise has the sadistic pirate aboard the *Fancy* off the Canary Islands where he is reported

Painting of Lowe

to have drowned when his ship sank in a violent storm with the loss of all hands.

Charles Harris

Buried on Goat Island, RI

In January of 1722 Charles Harris was First Mate and Navigator of the ship the *Greyhound* and was sailing from Honduras for Boston after loading with logwood.

Pirate Ship Attacks

The *Greyhound* was intercepted by Pirate Captain George Lowther and his ship the *Happy Delivery*.

They fought for 1 hour before the *Greyhound* stuck her colors and surrendered. The *Greyhound* was then boarded by pirates who, upon learning of the slim amount of wealth on board, started to bully and abuse the men.

Two men were tied to the mainmast and flogged until their backs were bloody messes; others were beaten about the face, head, and shoulders with the flats of the pirates' swords. Then everyone was taken aboard the *Happy Delivery*, and the *Greyhound* was set on fire.

Once aboard the pirate ship the Harris and four others agreed to sign the ship's articles and joined Lowther's crew. The rest were eventually put upon another ship attacked by Lowther.

Harris took to piracy like a fish to water. He made friends with Lowther and soon was given a ship of his own to command. For about 13 months he cruised and took prizes with Capt. Lowther and another pirate named Ned Low. They pillaged for quite a while and developed rather formidable reputations. Low in particular, as we have reported, was known to cut off prisoners' ears, lips, and noses, mash them and mix them into a kind of grotesque stew that he would then feed to other prisoners.

In 1722 Harris disappears for about 5 months, only to re-emerge off the coast of South Carolina in the sloop *Ranger*. He is once more in the company of Low who is sailing in a sloop called *Fortune*. On June 11th, 1723 off the coast of Long Island they were found by Capt. Solgard on the new *Greyhound* which was a fully armed Man of War. Capt. Solgard was a pirate hunter, and he was looking for Harris and Low in particular.

The pirates at first thought that they could easily outmatch the Greyhound, and started chasing after her. The chase and battle lasted from five in the morning until four in the afternoon. By that time the *Ranger* was badly damaged from the fight and was sitting dead in the water. When Low saw this he left Harris and his men for dead and sailed the *Fortune* away.

Harris surrendered and he and 48 of his crew were taken aboard the *Greyhound*. Of these men 30 were sent immediately to Newport for trial, 7 including Harris were taken to try and find Low, and the other 11 died from their wounds.

Low escaped capture from *Solgard*, and after a few weeks search Harris was also brought to Newport to stand trial. The trial was held in the Newport Colony House and Harris and 25 of his men were found guilty and sentenced to hang.

On July 19th 1723 most of Newport came to the area now know as Long Warf to watch the greatest mass hanging in RI's history. People either were picnicking in the field or were watching from their boats as each man was brought to the gallows. The bodies were then buried in an unmarked grave on the North end of Goat Island.

Philip Ashton

The real Robinson Crusoe hailed from Marblehead captured by Pirate Edward Lowe

Born in Marblehead, Massachusetts in 1702 he was the real life Robinson Crusoe who spent sixteen months as a castaway on Roatan Island in the Bay of Honduras in 1723/24. The book Robinson Crusoe, published in 1725 is said to be based upon Philip Ashton's adventure.

Philip was a fisherman who, while fishing off of the coast of Nova Scotia in June of 1723, was captured by the infamous Pirate Edward Lowe. Ten months later he managed to escape his captors by hiding in the jungle when they landed on a small deserted island to take on fresh water.

He was free from the grasp of his captors but had only the rags upon his back. Lacking tools, knife or weapons of any kind he could not hunt for game so he lived on fruits and berries.

Robinson Crusoe

Later he met an Englishman who mysteriously appeared out of the jungle, stayed a short while then dissapeared back into the jungle leaving behind a few tools, gun and gunpowder, tobacco and other supplies. His diet became more varied as he could now hunt game and make fire to cook a hot meal.

Ashton was finally rescued by the ship *Diamond* that hailed from Salem, Mass returning him safely home, May, 1st 1726 being gone nearly three years after his captured by pirates.

William Fly

Might he have been called "Black Fly"?

Captain William Fly was an English pirate who raided New England shipping until he was captured by the crew of a seized ship.

William Fly's career as a pirate began in April 1726 when he signed on to sail with Captain John Green to West Africa on the *Elizabeth*. Green and Fly began to clash until one night William led a mutiny that resulted in Capt. Green being tossed overboard. Fly then took command of the *Elizabeth*.

Having captured the ship, the mutineers sewed a Jolly Roger flag, renamed the ship *Fames' Revenge*, elected William Fly as captain, and sailed to the coast of North Carolina and north toward New England.

Gibbeted Pirate

They captured five ships in about two months before being captured themselves. Following his capture, Boston's Cotton Mather tried, and failed, to get Fly to publicly repent. William Fly and his crew were hanged at Boston Harbor on July 12, 1726. Reportedly, Fly approached the hanging with complete disdain and even reproached the hangman for doing a poor job, retying the noose and placing it about his neck with his own two hands. His last words were, roughly, a warning to captains to treat their sailors well and pay them on time. Following the hanging, his body was hung in chains (gibbeted) on Nixes' Mate Island in Boston Harbor, to serve as a warning to other sailors not to turn to piracy.

1726 Newspaper account of William Fly's short career as a pirate and his capture

Dated August 18. 1726

hurt.

Boſton, July 4. The Elizabeth Snow of Briſtol, John Green Commander, ſailing from Jamaica the latter End of April, or Beginning of May laſt, bound for Guinea, kept Company with the Fleet till he got through the Gulf of Florida. He loſt the Fleet one Morning, and the Night following his People on board, being Eleven in Number, all (except the Doctor, Carpenter, and Gunner) mutiny'd, and murder'd the Captain, and Chief Mate, and caſt them overboard on the 27th of May laſt. They then proceeded for the Coaſt of New England in a Pyratical Manner, taking ſeveral Veſſels, among which was a Snow from North Carolina, bound to this Place, taken by them the 3d of June, on board of which Sloop was one William Atkinſon a Paſſenger, who was detain'd by them to navigate their Snow (they not having any Navigator on board.) After which they took a Scooner belonging to Marblehead; and having put on board of it ſeven of their Gang, they left the Snow, commanded by Captain Fly, (who was Captain Green's Boatſwain when murder'd) he having then but three reputed Pyrates with him, the reſt being forced Men. On the 23d of June kinſon taking this Advantage, with the Aſſiſtance of more forced Men, ſurprized and ſecured Fly and his

203

Legend of Nix's Mate Island

Nixes Mate, also known as Nixes Island, Nix's Mate and Nick's Mate, is a very small island in the Boston Harbor Islands National Recreation Area. The island is situated about 6 miles offshore of downtown Boston. The island is only 200 square feet in size and rises to a height of 10 feet above sea level.

A prominent black and white wooden pyramid beacon, resting atop a granite base, increases the island's height to 20 feet. The base was erected by Boston Marine Society in 1805 and is managed by the United States Coast Guard.

In 1726, upon the arrest of William Fly, the infamous pirate, officials brought him to Boston where he was executed. His body was then gibbeted (Hanged in an iron cage) on Nixes Mate to serve as a warning to sailors not to turn to piracy.

Before Fly's execution, he famously scolded the hangman for incorrectly securing his noose. His body as well as those of two other pirates were buried on the island.

Wait a minute, how could you possibly bury three persons on an island the equivalent in size to a 10' X 20' shed and still have room to perform executions?

The answer to that question lies in the island's name. Before it was called Nix's Mate the island bore the name of its owner a Mr. Gallop who used the then sizable island for the grazing of his sheep. Who was Captain Nix's mate and why was this island named after him?

The Curse of Nix's Mate

History has not recorded the name of Captain Nix's hapless mate. What is known is that he was accused of a capital crime of which he vehemently professed his innocence. His protestations were ignored by all and he was taken out to the then 12 acre island that would later reference his life.

It was the custom in the 1700s to hang pirates and other maritime criminals on this island located on the starboard side of the main channel into Boston Harbor. They were to hang there to illustrate and to serve as an example to all approaching Boston from away of the severe punishment metered out to wrong doers.

Pirate gibbeted on Nix's Mate

Can you imagine the reaction of weary immigrants as they arrived in Boston Harbor being greeted by corpses blow in in the wind! Certainly not the welcoming message the Statue of Liberty would portray two hundred fifty miles south and one hundred years later.

Before the hangman sprung the trap door that would send Nix's mate into eternity and posterity he screamed a curse into the salty wind: "I curse this island and those who condemn me and this island will disappear beneath the sea in proof of my innocence."

Remarkably the island began to diminish in size and before too long it would have been completely under water if the granite base had not been constructed to hold a channel marker and beacon. Was this proof of Nix's mate's innocence, or was the disappearance of the island just a coincidence?

George and Rachel Wall

Boston's husband and wife pirate team

She was the last woman to be hanged in Boston.

Rachael was born Rachel Schmidt on a farm outside of Carlisle, PA sometime in the late 1750s.

She eloped with and married George Wall when she was about sixteen and they moved to Boston where she was a chamber-maid on Beacon Hill and he a fisherman.

George signed aboard a privateer during the American Revolution and was there exposed to the life of a privateer, which is essentially a pirate with a Letter of Marque.

After four years as a privateer George and a few compatriots stole a sloop in Essex, MA. They established a base of operation pretending to

Pirates board unsuspecting rescuers

be a family of fishermen, on Appledore Island, part of the Isles of Shoals, off the Maine, New Hampshire coast.

They concocted a very devious plan that proved equally effective and ruthless. They would set their small sloop adrift in the path of ship traffic with George and the other men hiding below decks leaving the lovely young Rachael alone topside. When a passing ship came within earshot Rachael would begin her 'Damsel in Distress" act by running up the distress flag and screaming for help at the top of her lungs.

When the unsuspecting rescuers came along side the men would spring from their hiding places and capture the ship, pillage anything of value then kill the crew and sink their vessel.

The plan depended upon stealth and deception and therefore no survivors could be allowed, no evidence of their wicked piracy could be permitted to remain. Accordingly, all must die and every ship plundered must be sunk without leaving a trace.

From 1781 through the fall of 1782 this husband and wife pirate team sank scores of ships, murdered dozens of men and stole thousands of dollars worth of booty. Their plan apparently worked as everyone on shore assumed the missing ships were lost at sea, as was common in the period.

The Wall's good luck streak came to an end in the guise of a hurricane in the fall of 1782 when George and his men were washed overboard and drowned. Rachael was the sole survivor and ironically, was now indeed a damsel truly in need of rescue. She was saved from the raging sea and returned to Boston.

Rachael retired from piracy and returned to her former occupation as a housemaid and soon resorted to stealing and pilfering to augment her meager income and perhaps add a bit of excitement to her now comparatively dull existence.

In 1789 she was caught attacking a seventeen year old girl on the Boston streets and stealing her bonnet. She was

Rachel Wall on the gallows

arrested, tried and on September 10, 1789 found guilty. At this time she confessed to being a pirate and wished to be tried as such. Her wish was denied and she was hung for robbery and was reportedly the last women to be executed by hanging in the Commonwealth of Massachusetts.

Charles Gibbs

His last words "No mercy did we ever show for dead men can tell no tales"

Charles Gibbs, a Rhode Island native, was born into a respectable family. His real name was James D. Jeffers and was one of the last executed for piracy in the United States. Charles was an incorrigible child, expelled from school and addicted to fiendish and cruel behavior. At age 15 he went to sea aboard the US sloop of war, *Hornet* and later became a prisoner of war and was confined in Dartmoor Prison.

He returned to Rhode Island after a prisoner exchange and borrowed money to open a retail store he called the *Tin Pot*.

Reportedly it was "a place full of abandoned women and dissolute fellows." Although called a grocery store, he dealt primarily in liquor as he had a "*License to retail Spirits*, and his drunkery was thronged with customers." He soon went out of business and returned to the sea.

Crew mutinies

He joined the privateer *John* as a seaman and sailed south. During this cruise, the crew mutinied. He took command of the ship and headed to the West Indies in search of their fortune. Soon they had captured more than twenty ships murdering nearly four hundred people in the process.

Havana was the port of call where pirates could exchange their plunder for gold and silver. It was here that Gibbs and his fellow cutthroats found themselves trapped by the British sloop of war, *Jearus*. After a prolonged battle Gibbs and his fellow pirates escaped ashore and hid in the mountains, leaving behind twelve vessels burned to the water line and their crews of one hundred fifty men murdered. Dead men tell no tales.

Gibbs traveled the world for several years living the high life in New York, Boston and London until his blood money ran out, and he eventually returned to Boston.

From Boston, Gibbs took passage as a seaman aboard the brig *Vineyard* bound for New Orleans. On the return trip, Gibbs convinced a few shipmates to mutiny, seize the ship and the money they were convinced the captain had secreted aboard. True to his bloody style, Gibbs murdered the captain and first mate in the dark of night and threw their bodies into the black sea. The crew elected Gibbs captain and they set course for Long Island.

They divided the kegs of money amongst the crew. Each share amounted to more than five thousand dollars. Gibbs developed a plan. They would scuttle the ship far at sea in the dark of night and the crew, with their money, would row ashore in the ship's two small boats and walk away rich men.

Pirates bury money on Barron Island

The two boats were approaching land just before daybreak when they both ran up upon a bar. The boats began taking on water. Their boats foundered, filled with water and about $50,000 in money was lost. They made landfall on Barron Island and proceeded to bury the remaining money. It is reported that the money was never retrieved by Gibbs and remains to be found.

Gibbs and his mate Wansley were captured and tried at New York for piracy and murder and were pronounced guilty on March 11, 1831.

Gibbs Confesses to Murders and Rape

During his imprisonment, Gibbs boldly confessed to murdering hundreds of men, women and children in cold blood.

Perhaps the most horrific event recounted by Gibbs involves an innocent and beautiful young girl of about seventeen who he forced to watch her parents and all of the other passengers, man, woman, boy and girl - butchered before her eyes. Her demise was delayed for dark and nefarious reasons. According to Gibbs - "she received such treatment, the bare recollection of which causes me to shudder!"

Gibbs abducts teen age girl

The pirates took her from the ship to a small fort at the west end of Cuba and confined her there for about two months. Finally, she was taken aboard ship where it was decided that, for the safety of all concerned (except that of the girl) she would be put to death. The pirates poisoned her and summarily threw her lifeless body overboard. Apparently, they believed that dead girls as well as dead men would tell no tales.

On October 21, 1821, while his fleet of four ships was attacking three merchantmen off Cape Antonio, Cuba, the brig USS *Enterprise* under Lieutenant Commander Lawrence Kearny came upon the scene. Despite outnumbering the USS *Enterprise,* Gibbs's fleet was destroyed after a short battle and he was forced to flee into the jungle with his surviving crew.

Little is known about his life immediately following this escape. He claimed to have resided in the United States by 1825, and to have served Argentina in the Cisplatine War as both a regular naval officer and as commander of a privateer. Following a reputed voyage to North Africa to join the Barbary Corsairs, Gibbs was eventually forced to find work as a sailor again.

After signing with the brig *Vineyard* he and Thomas J. Wansley led a mutiny, killing the captain and his first mate on the night of November 23, 1830 in order to seize its cargo of silver.

The mutineers headed for Long Island where they scuttled the vessel and came ashore, several mutineers losing their lives in rough waters which also claimed much of their loot. After only a few days ashore Gibbs, Wansley, and two others were captured and taken to prison in New York City where he and Wansley were tried and convicted of mutiny and murder in 1831.

They were incarcerated at Bridewell Prison, then moved to Bellevue Prison and were hanged at Ellis Island on April 22, 1831. Gibbs' skull is on display in the museum of the General Society of Mechanics and Tradesmen.

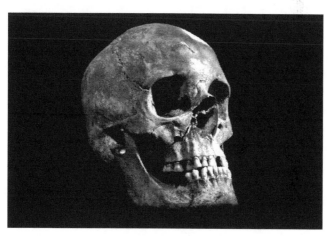

Skull on display

Edward (Seegar) England

His "Jolly Roger" is the Classic Pirate Flag

Edward England, born Edward Seegar in Ireland, was a famous African coast and Indian Ocean pirate from 1717 to 1720. The ships he sailed on included the *Pearl* and later the *Fancy*, for which England exchanged the *Pearl* in 1720.

His flag was the classic Jolly Roger with a skull above two crossed thigh bones on a black background.

Captain England's Jolly Roger

He differed from many other pirates of his day in that he did not kill captives unless it was absolutely necessary. However, this ultimately led to his downfall, for his crew mutinied against him when he refused to kill sailors from the *Cassandra*, an English trading ship, captained by James Macrae.

He was subsequently marooned on Mauritius with two other crew members, where they fashioned a small raft and made it to St. Augustine's Bay in Madagascar. England survived for a short while by begging for food and died around the end of 1720.

212

Where Treasure Has Been Found in New England

Locations Where Pirates are Said to Have Buried Treasure

Money Head on Hog Island, Pleasant Bay, Cape Cod

Captain Kidd, according to local tradition, buried his gold at Money Head on Hog Island in Pleasant Bay, off Orleans. Several places on the Atlantic coast claim the honor of harboring the booty. Many pirate historians consider Cape Cod's Hog Island as one of the most likely places to find hidden treasure.

The southern end of Hog Island is known locally as "Money Head," and a large rock and hole once found there are referred to as evidence of repeated excavations.

Hog Island lies deserted in Pleasant Bay. Only the adventurous seek its shores. You can row over and inspect the diggings. You may even pick up an abandoned spade, but you are not advised to use it till you know the lore of treasure trove.

Once a year only, it is whispered in Orleans, do you stand a chance of finding Captain Kidd's treasure – only on the seventh night of the seventh month with a full moon at Money Head. There at the stroke of midnight you slay a sheep and let the blood flow from the cut to the spot where the gold is buried, and you start digging... It is said Captain Kidd stored his treasure: ..."in a box, lockt and nailed, corded and sealed."

Hannah Screecham - the Witch of Grand Island - Cape Cod

Hannah Screecham and her sister Sarah lived on what was formerly called Sampson Island and now is Grand Island off the town of Cotuit near Mashpee. Sarah moved to south Mashpee and made her home on what now is called "Witches Pond." She was considered to be a witch by the townsfolk and so they left her alone. Hannah stayed to live alone on the island.

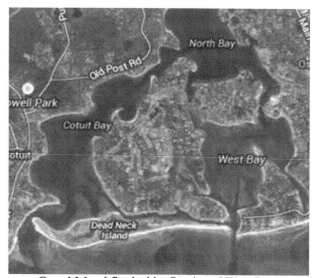

Grand Island flanked by Cotuit and West Bays

Grand Island is flanked by West Bay and Cotuit Bay. Grand Island is reported to have been a favorite pirate haven because the bays provide the best shelter from storms on the south side of the Cape. Accordingly, Hannah was in a fine position to befriended many pirates such as Blackbeard, Captain William Kidd, Black Sam Bellamy and many others.

One legend retells of Hannah helping Captain Kidd bury treasure in the dunes of Grand Island. She is said to have directed one of Kidd's crewmen to dig a deep hole into which the chests of gold, silver, jewels and other treasure would be placed. Once the task had been completed Hannah is said to have struck the sailor on the head with a shovel and, laughing her satanic laugh, pushed his unconscious body into the hole and buried him alive. Hannah's laugh was said to sound like an

215

enraged seagull and would send a chill up the spine of the fiercest pirate. This unfortunate sailor was not her first victim nor would he be her last.

A second version of the tale is that the pirates murdered Hannah and buried her body along with the treasure to act as the protector of the treasure. It is believed that her ghost would

Pirate burying treasure

prevent anyone from digging up the treasure.

No one has found any more than a single Spanish piece of eight on Grand Island however, where there is one can many more be far away? Some say no treasure has been found because it so well guarded by the witch Hannah Screecham. Is that the cry of a seagull you hear on Grand Island or is it the ghost of Hannah Screecham?

Nomansland Island

Another local spot rumored to be where some of Kidd's booty was stashed is Nomans Land Island (aka Nomansland Island). An uninhabited island off of Cape Cod and south of Martha's Vineyard's Gay Head.

One local legend relates the tale of a mysterious stranger who arrived in the Elizabeth Islands about seventy years after Kidd's death. He was an old sailor, and he said that he had sailed with Captain Kidd as a young lad, and that he had personally assisted in burying the treasure on Nomansland Island.

The rickety old sailor attempted to draw out a map - but died before he finished the document. Residents of Robinson's Hole, where the man died, set out to find the treasure. But they were never able to find it.

Gardiners Island –
South of Cape Cod

Capt'n Kidd buried treasure on the island in June, 1699, having stopped there while sailing to Boston to answer charges of piracy. With the permission of the island's proprietor, he buried a chest and a box of gold and two boxes of silver in a ravine between Bostwick's Point and the Manor House. The box of gold, Kidd told Gardiner, was intended for Lord Bellomont.

For Mrs. Gardiner's trouble he gave her a length of gold cloth captured from a Moorish ship off Madagascar, and a sack of sugar. A piece of the cloth is now on display at the East Hampton library and a stone plaque marks the spot where the treasure was found.

Plaque

Kidd was tried in Boston, and Gardiner was ordered by Governor Bellomont to deliver the treasure as evidence. The booty included gold dust, bars of silver, Spanish dollars, rubies, diamonds, candlesticks, and porringers. Gardiner kept one of the diamonds which he later gave to his daughter.

Smuttynose Island

Smuttynose is one of the Isles of Shoals, located 6 miles north of Cape Cod off the coast of New Hampshire, but actually is in the state of Maine. It was named by fishermen, seeing the island at sea level and noticing how the profuse seaweed at one end looked like the "smutty nose" of some vast sea animal.

Reports are that Blackbeard and other pirates buried treasure here, some of which has been found. Blackbeard never took marriage seriously & during his lifetime he had fourteen wives & fathered forty children. In 1691, he & a sizeable crew landed at Lunging Island in the Isles of Shoals off Portsmouth, New Hampshire. There he buried a large treasure of silver bars six of which have been discovered. Blackbeard used the island as location to rendezvous with his other pirate captains.

Silver Ingots Found

Capt. Sam Haley found five silver ingots on Smuttynose Island in 1820, which he used to pay for the construction of the breakwater. Pieces of eight are reportedly buried somewhere near the Smuttynose breakwater.

During W.W.II, people living on Londoner Island saw government officials searching the crescent-shaped beach facing Star Island with radio locators and probes. In the 1950s, various newspapers printed aerial photographs that allegedly showed that metal, probably precious, was present on one of the islands. A company was established to hunt for treasure there, but nothing reportedly came of it. Lunging, Star, and White Islands have all been named as other sites where a lost treasure has be hidden and might be found.

One story has it that Sandy Gordon, captain of the Flying Scot and a Blackbeard confederate, split the treasure taken from a Spanish galleon with his men while on Star Island, buried his portion of the loot on White Island, and left his girl friend Martha there to guard it. Soon after, he was killed in a battle with a British warship. On stormy nights, Martha's ghost supposedly haunts the island, which could lead one to believe that the treasure is still there.

Legends of Treasure

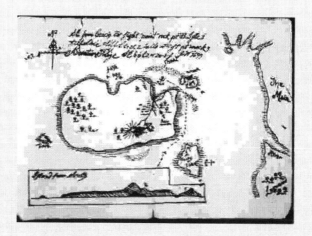

Where it Might be Found

Legends of Treasure on Cape Cod

Horseneck Beach

Many men have searched for the treasure of the famous pirate, Captain Kidd. At least one man, James M. Eddy, had a measure of success. While searching for Captain Kidd's treasure, Eddy ultimately found a pirate treasure buried by someone else.

Eddy owned a farm adjoining Horseneck Beach. In 1886, a parchment treasure map came into his possession. Though he would not say how he got the map, some of Eddy's friends and neighbors speculated that his grandfather had either been a pirate, or had been involved with pirates. They believed the

grandfather passed the map down to Eddy's father, and that Eddy had inherited it from him. Eddy denied that his grandfather or any of his relatives were ever connected with pirates.

Dunes at Horseneck Beach

Apparently, the map was made from a piece of parchment that had served as a drumhead. The lines on the map seemed to have been drawn with a sharp, pointed object. The map supposedly showed the locations of three separate caches of gold, silver, and other treasures buried by the pirates many years before. A large rock on Horseneck Point served as the starting point. At the time this was an isolated area.

After obtaining the map, Eddy conducted his treasure hunting secretly. He began at the large rock in the Summer of 1886. A full year later, he dug up a kettle filled with old Spanish silver coins. The coins were dated from 1781 to 1851, ruling out the possibility that they were part of Captain Kidd's much-sought treasure as Kidd was hanged in London on May 24, 1701.

According to the map, one of the other caches contained gold coins, while another held diamonds and jewels. There are no records indicating whether Eddy ever found these caches. A search of old land titles would reveal the location of Eddy's farm. If there is any pirate treasure left, it should be nearby.

Andrea Dorias

According to the *Andrea Dorias* papers, when she sank off Cape Cod in 1956, her safe deposit boxes contained over $750,000 in money and jewels. In the pursers safe there

The Sinking Made Headlines

was $250,000 in American and Italian money.

Chatham Light

In 1831, a fisherman named Arthur Doane found a fortune in Spanish gold on Cape Cod. He kept his treasure secret for 49 years, and then, on his deathbed, finally told a friend.

However, the friend did not recover all of the treasure. Most of it is still buried somewhere in the silvery sand of Cape Cod, not far from the old Chatham Light, where a few scattered gold coins are found from time to time.

In 1831, Arthur Doane had seen pirates bury several chests of treasure near Chatham. Digging the chests up, Doane reburied the money. He then made a deal to sell a few coins at a time to a friend. This transaction went on for 49 years.

When Doane became ill in 1880, he told his friend where the other chests were buried. But a storm, as fate would have it, came up that night, and his friend stayed inside. Doane died that night and his friend never was able to locate the remaining chests of money. Many have searched for this buried treasure, but its location has never been found.

221

Six Bags of Chatham Gold

Another version of the Doane Legend reports that in 1831 a fisherman, who lived near the Chatham Lighthouse, had six bags of gold that he is said to have salvaged from a wreck on one of Cape Cod's shifting sand bars. He kept the find a secret from everyone, including his family until, on his death bed, he revealed where he had hid the gold to his only surviving relative.

The gold he said, is to be found "buried 50 rods due north of Chatham Lighthouse, near a large Scrub Pine." The relative didn't really believe the story so didn't look very hard or long to find the treasure. Instead, he preferred to relish in re-telling his relative's death bed story framed as the last gasps of a deranged old fisherman.

Chatham Light today

Mobile Lighthouses – Chatham's Twin Lights

A bit of history: Two twin octagonal 40 ft wooden towers, known as Chatham Twin Lights, were built in 1808, many years before the fisherman's death. They were built in order to distinguish the Chatham Lighthouses from Highland Light, the first Cape Cod light, and to act as range lights.

Sailors would line up the range lights, one being taller than the other, until they were vertically aligned and follow the line into the harbor. The two structures were on skids so that they could be moved to keep them in line with the entrance channel as its sandy entrance shifted.

In 1923 the northern tower of the pair was moved roughly 12 miles north to become the first Nauset Light

The facts that: the two lighthouses could move, that one had been removed plus - it is unlikely that the same Scrub Pine is still there almost two hundred years later, complicates following the fisherman's directions to locating the six bags of gold.

Is the gold still buried somewhere near Chatham Lighthouse? Are the occasional gold coins found in the area a clue? Do you own a metal detector?

King of Calf Island

The reason this story is worth investigating is that $1,900 of the reported $500,000 has already been found. The first mention of treasure and Calf Island was in 1882.

In 1846, a man took a job as keeper of Bug Light in Boston Harbor. Although he lived quietly, the story leaked out that he was an ex-pirate in hiding. After several years, the lighthouse keeper retired and moved to one of the outer harbor islands. He lived here, and was called the King of Calf Island, until his death in 1882.

Just after the turn of the last century, a Canadian conducted a search for treasure on Greater Brewster Island, just off Boston. One Pegleg Nuskey passed this information on in 1937, to Edward Snow, a writer in the Boston area.

Pirate Booty

Before Snow could act on the information, he was suddenly actively involved in World War II.

Snow completed his hitch in 1944, and began to think again about the King of Calf Island. Here is one version of what transpired thereafter:

Somehow Snow got the idea that the King must have left a chart showing the exact location of his treasure, which was supposed to be worth about $500,000. He didn't find the chart, but he did get hold of an old book in Italian which local tradition said had belonged to the King. Snow took the book to the Boston Public Library for appraisal.

Now comes the part of the story that reads like fiction, but the facts were reported by the Boston papers and retold in *Time Magazine*, on October 15, 1945. According to *Time*s account, the old Italian book was turned over to Harriet Swift of the Boston Public Library. She turned the leaves and noticed a pattern of pin-holes on page 101. The holes pierced letters, forming a simple coded message.

Secret Message

The exciting message: The King of Calf Island had buried a treasure on Strong Island, off the shore of Cape Cod.

When this coded message was explained to him, Edward Snow and his brother Donald set out for Strong Island at once. The pin pricks evidently did not tell exactly where the stuff was buried, but Snow took along a metal detector.

Metal Detector to find treasure

The Snow brothers dug five holes in the sand, and each time they found metal; but it proved to be only iron from some old wreck. But in the sixth excavation they hit the jackpot, according to *Time*, when the men unearthed a small, encrusted copper box. It was full of tarnished old coins, minted in Peru, Mexico, Portugal, France, and Spain. *Time* magazine carried a picture of Edward Snow sitting in the sand, with the box open in front of him, and both hands full of coins. The treasure amounted to only about $1,900.

While this was quite a treasure in 1945, the big question to a modern-day treasure hunter is, where is the remaining supposed $498,000 that the King of Calf Island is believed to have hidden? As far as can be learned, nothing else has been found.

Nauset Beach

The beaches along this stretch are known to produce a large number of coins and other artifacts, especially after significant storms.

From which of the hundreds of shipwrecks that have occurred off this beach does the the treasure come is impossible to know. We do know that the only pirate ship loaded with tons of gold, silver and jewels ever found was recently located just a few yards off Marconi Beach.

You can be sure you are at the beach where the Whydah went when you see the sign posted on the railing leading down to the beach which reads; "No Metal Detectors Allowed."

Treasure buried in the sand?

Pirate battle
By Howard Pyle -1898

Treasure on the Isles of Shoals

Choice of Pirates for Centuries

The islands that comprise the Isle of Shoals: Star Island, Appledore Island, Smuttynose Island, White Island, Cedar Island, Duck Island, Lunging Island, Eastern Island, Shag Island , Mingo Island and Seavey Island, have been reported to have been favored by pirates since the 1600's.

Smuttynose Island, at 25 acres, is the third-largest island. It is known as the site of Blackbeard's honeymoon, later for the shipwreck of the Spanish ship *Sagunto* in 1813,

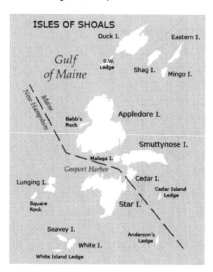

Malaga Island is a diminutive island just to the west of Smuttynose, connected to it by a breakwater.

That breakwater was built around 1820 by Captain Samuel Haley, who is reputed to have paid for its construction with proceeds from four bars of pirate silver that he found under a flat rock on the island.

We have collected several legendary accounts of piratical activity in these islands. Many of the legends have been supported by the finds of gold and silver coins as well as silver bars.

How much treasure has been found and not reported will never be known.

We have compiled a collection of the island's legends of pirates and treasure

Spanish Galleon Runs Aground on Star Island

Some early records from Spain indicate that a Spanish galleon had crashed on the eastern shore of Star Island around 1685, at a spot known as Miss Underhill's Chair. This galleon carried a substantial amount of gold coins, silver place, and silver bullion. Incidentally, the Cosport Church,

Spanish Galleon

located on Star Island, was constructed partly of timbers from this galleon.

On the western side of the island there was once an old fort that was protected by nine cannons. Although the cannons have since been removed, the area of the fort itself is a good site for to search for relics, coins, and the like.

Silver Ship Disaster

In the 18th century, Appledore Island was the scene of a terrible silver ship disaster in which sailors managed to get ashore with a substantial amount of the bullion that had been aboard. The history of the sailors has been lost in the years, but there have been many cases of people finding silver coins on or near the ledges along the eastern side of the island.

Blackbeard Buries Treasure on Smuttynose

Smuttynose Island reportedly is the site of Blackbeard's buried treasure of silver bars and pieces-of-eight. The silver bars are believed to be the same ones found by a Captain Samuel Haley. Haley found five large silver bars while building a sea wall for Malaga Island. So if, indeed, those were the silver bars Blackbeard buried, then the pieces-of-eight are yet to be found.

Shipwreck on Smuttynose Yields Gold and Silver

In January 1813 a ship named *Conception* out of Cadiz, Spain, was far off its course in a storm and slid by Cedar Island and crashed ashore at Southeast Point, Smuttynose Island. Her cargo of dried fruits, almonds, bales of broadcloth, and a treasure of gold and silver went down with her crew. Considerable gold and silver was discovered shortly after the wreck on the low-tide shore. Also found was a silver pocket watch inscribed with the initials P. S.

Pirate John Quelch Secrets Treasure on White Island

White Island, which is one mile southwest of Star Island, also holds treasure buried by John Quelch and probably others at several locations on the island.

How much of Quelch's treasure is buried on the Isles of Shoals is open to conjecture. *Life Magazine*, in 1950, stated that $100,000 was buried there, about half of which has been recovered. In "1001 Lost, Buried, or Sunken Treasures", the authoritative F. L. Coffman said that Quelch's crew secreted $275,000 on Star Island and established several other caches on White Island.

Originally a pirate hunter, John Quelch turned pirate when the opportunity presented itself. In July 1703, he signed aboard the brigantine *Charles of Boston*, which was outfitted as a privateer to sail against the French in Nova Scotia and Newfoundland waters. The captain of the boat was a man named Daniel Plowman.

Captain Plowman was unhappy, however, with the caliber of the crew which was recruited to man the newly-built, eighty-ton craft. To make matters worse, he was taken ill just before the ship was set to sail.

Anthony Holding, one of the crew's ringleaders, assumed command. He locked the ailing captain in his cabin and ordered the ship out to sea. Once underway, the crew chose John Quelch to be the captain, probably because he had the most knowledge of navigation. Instead of sailing northeast to battle the French ships, the *Charles* now set a course to the south on a search for plunder in the Caribbean and the Spanish Main. Sometime after Quelch had assumed command, Captain Plowman was thrown overboard, but whether dead or alive is not known.

Captain Sent Overboard

During the next three months Quelch made nine captures, five brigantines, a small sloop, two fishing boats, and a ship of about two hundred tons. These vessels were the property of the subjects of the King of Portugal, now an ally of the Queen of England. From these ships Quelch secured rich booty including a hundred-weight of gold dust, gold, and silver coins to the value of over one thousand pounds, ammunition, small arms, and a great quantity of fine fabrics, provisions, and rum. By attacking these ships, Quetch became a pirate, and the English Navy was on the watch for him.

Quelch arrived back at Marblehead, Massachusetts, where he was eventually arrested. However, between the time of his arrival and his arrest, he and several members of his crew managed to make their way to Star Island and White Island and bury large sums of money which they had obtained while in the Caribbean.

Quelch was arrested and sentenced to death by hanging. On June 30, 1704, he was hung at the foot of Fleet Street in Boston, Massachusetts. He took the knowledge of the location of his buried treasure with him into eternity.

The Legend of Pirate Sandy Gordon's White Isle Treasure

Captain Sandy Gordon, a pirate who buried a huge treasure sometime between 1715 and 1718 on White Island has been best described as both mean and greedy. White Island is one of nine small outcroppings of rock which are the Isles of Shoals and are found about ten miles off the shores of both Maine and New Hampshire.

Gordon went to sea from his home in Scotland while still a boy. The first record of his nautical career was as a ship's carpenter aboard the *Porpoise,* an armed merchantman commanded by Captain John Herring. The captain was commissioned to capture Algerian corsairs who were creating havoc with British shipping in the area of the Barbary Coast.

Captain Has Daughter Aboard

Captain's Daughter

It was against all nautical protocols of the day, but Captain Herring took his beautiful eighteen-year-old daughter Martha on this mission rather than leave her alone at home.

The *Porpoise* was not out of London but a few days when young Gordon began to make serious advances toward the golden-haired young maiden. Captain Herring soon caught wind of this and told Gordon to back off or face the venom of the cat-o-nine-tails.

The young ship's carpenter heeded this warning for a few days, but Martha's beauty attracted him like a powerful magnet. In fact, it was not long thereafter that Captain Herring trapped Gordon alone with the girl in the captain's cabin.

The father was furious. Seizing the young seaman by the throat, he threw him sprawling upon the deck and sentenced him to seventy-two lashes upon his bare back. In addition, he was clapped into irons and interred in the ships hold for thirty days to meditate over his amorous activity.

When he finally returned to duty, Sandy went about his appointed tasks quietly and diligently, but this was only on the surface. Clandestinely, he was plotting a bold mutiny with certain unsavory members of the crew. As soon as a majority of the hands were ready to challenge Captain Herring, the conspiracy was ripe.

Mutiny on the Porpoise

Gordon selected a dark night when he was on watch. At a shot from Gordon's pistol, the mutineers seized control of the *Porpoise*, overwhelming Captain Herring and the loyal crewmen. The surprised master was hauled from his cabin and bound to a cannon.

The punishment that Captain Herring had so recently meted out to Sandy was all too indelibly printed on the young sailor's mind. Seizing a lash, he evened the score then and there with seventy-two strokes upon the master's back. After several such beatings, spaced one hour apart, the Captain finally died and Gordon threw his body overboard.

Become a Pirate or be Thrown Overboard

At this point, Sandy locked Martha in the captain's cabin and forbade anyone to approach her. He gave everyone on board a choice, either turn pirate or be thrown overboard. The choice was easy to make. It was at this time that Gordon showed his greedy nature. His policy on this pirate ship was that there would be no division of plunder, as was the custom among buccaneers. All profits would be his. One slight concession was made, that the men would be paid wages twenty-five percent higher than those on merchant ships.

Fired as Captain, Expelled from the Ship

Now under the Jolly Roger, the ship sailed for some time off the coast of Scotland, capturing several valuable prizes. However, the crew grew exasperated with Gordon's reaping all the profits while they risked life and limb. So it was not unexpected when they rebelled against Gordon. As a result, the pirates set Sandy and Martha adrift in a small boat and let them row for the Scottish coast. The two managed to find an old farm house as their home in the desolate coastal area.

Enter Blackbeard

It was at that time that the rascally Captain Edward Teach, a/k/a Blackbeard, and a small party visited this lonely shore in search of water, food, and liquor. When Blackbeard came upon Gordon's humble abode, the latter did not have much to offer except lurid tales of his prowess as an adventurer and one-time pirate.

Pirates do battle

Come aboard my ship, said Blackbeard, and I'll see how good a pirate you are. If you are as good as your boasting, I'll see you outfitted, and maybe we can do business together.

Soon after Gordon came aboard, the pirates sighted a richly laden East Indian ship, homeward bound for London. Harold T. Wilkins in his book "Pirate Treasure" relates that the merchant ship put up a furious defense.

Made Captain by Blackbeard

Gordon fought like a wild beast with cutlass and pistol until the merchantman's deck was clear of defenders. When the prize was finally secure, Blackbeard slapped Gordon on the back and announced, Good work, lad. By your bravery today ye shown that ye deserve to be skipper of this prize. But mind you, all loot will be shared with the crew.

Thus it was that Gordon renamed the ship the *Flying Scot*, and he and Blackbeard set sail for the Spanish Main. This cruise was highly successful with both ships being well loaded with plunder. Eventually the two ships parted company, with an agreement to meet again at a future date among the Isles of Shoals.

Stopped to Pick up his Girlfriend

Following this agreement, Gordon sailed back to Scotland where he dropped anchor near his coastal farmhouse. He went ashore in a small boat and returned to his ship in the darkness of that night with the beautiful Martha in his arms. She was bound and carried kicking and screaming to the ship. Not a good way to begin the long journey to America.

On the cruise to America, the *Flying Scot* sighted a great Spanish galleon and gave chase. As the pirates drew near, the Spaniard let go with a broadside which was inaccurate enough to cause little damage. Meanwhile, the *Flying Scot* lived up to her name and pulled alongside the Spaniard. Grappling hooks were thrown to link the ships together, and then the buccaneers swarmed aboard their victim like a host of angry hornets.

Gordon played it safe and stood on his quarterdeck until his men had the situation well in hand. Now the time had come for him to leap aboard the merchantman and take the Spanish captain as his prisoner.

The galleons captain proved to be a very stubborn individual, but, after some highly persuasive measures, he revealed the amount of treasure on board and the secret places in which it was stored, and then he was thrown overboard. Gordon took more than a million dollars worth of gold and silver out of the Spanish vessel.

His crew Buried their Loot on Star Island

The *Flying Scot* arrived at the Isles of Shoals several weeks before Captain Teach. Landing at Star Island, Gordon ordered a division of the treasure to be made. When this had been accomplished, *the crew broke up into several small groups to bury their shares of loot.*

What of Captain Gordon and the fair Martha? They took up residence a short distance away on White Island. Sandy had a

Star Island at Isle of Shoals

small cottage built for them there, and it was near the cottage that he buried his treasure.

How much did he bury? This is anyone's guess, but most authorities agree that it was an amount of considerable value.

In time, Blackbeard arrived on the scene, and there was more burying of treasure. Blackbeard is alleged to have cached as much as $300,000 on Star Island. Both he and Gordon held several conferences at this time, and when it was amicably agreed to dissolve their partnership, Blackbeard took off for the Spanish Main.

Unfortunate Case of Mistaken Identity

A week or two later, a lookout spied a sail on the horizon. The lure for more booty was great, so Gordon hastily assembled the crew and lifted anchor. The strange sail turned out to be a British man-o-war on a hunt for pirates. A long and fierce conflict followed in which the British ship finally silenced Gordon's guns. The vessels were locked together for the last stage of the conflict, when a tremendous explosion rent the air, strewing the sea with the fragments of both ships.

Stung to madness by defeat and knowing that, if taken alive, he would be gallows bait, Sandy Gordon fired the *Flying Scots* magazine, sending himself and his merry men to eternity. His girlfriend and his treasure remained on White Island.

Appledore Island – The "legend of Old Babs"

Located in the Isles of Shoals, this island was another treasure hiding-place. According to local legend, Captain Kidd hid some of his treasure here and put one of his crew to death that he might haunt the place and frighten searchers away, keeping the treasure's location forever secret.

For years no fisherman could be induced to land on the island after nightfall. It is said that a gaze from "Old Bab's" (supposedly the ghost of Capt. Kidd's murdered crewman) dreadful face would scared a sailor to death. The legend is that an islander once encounter "Old Bab" while out and about one night. He is reported to have seen "Old Bab" with a glowing phosphorescence gleaming from his ghostly body. His family found his dead body the next morning.

Old Bab's dreadful face?

Did the unfortunate islander stroll too close to Captain Kidd's treasure for "Old Bab's" comfort or; did he simply have a sudden and fatal heart attack?

The Blood Red Rubies of Boon Island – Isle of Shoals

September 25, 1710, the English ship *Nottingham* departed her home port of London and headed for New England. The 120 ton Galley was crewed by fourteen men and carried ten cannon and was commanded by Captain Jonathan Dean. Her cargo consisted of: loads of cordwood, butter and cheese from Ireland, plus one very special cargo, a packet of twelve blood-red rubies in the charge of agent Winthrop Sloan, the sole passenger aboard.

Only in America

They were sold to a wealthy French aristocrat, the Count de Florent, on the condition that they be rendered into matching items of jewelry that matched those of a large pendant and brooch he owned. The Count insisted that the only person in the world capable of performing the task was a goldsmith living in America so off to America went the precious rubies.

Red rubies

The rubies were quite large and carefully packed into an oblong metal box measuring one inch by one-half inch by twelve inches. The box was then securely stored in the ships iron safe. The stones estimated market value today would be well in excess of $1,500,000.

As the *Nottingham* approached New England she was firmly gripped by blinding December snow storm and a full-force gale. The heavy wind threatened to capsize the ship, so Captain Dean ordered the sails dropped. However, before the task could be completed, a huge wave lifted the galley and plunged it against the eastern end of the jagged, exposed rock known as Boon Island.

237

Miraculously everyone had survived the sinking, including the passenger Sloan. As the splintered *Nottingham* and her ruby treasure vanished beneath the boiling waves, the men settled into prayer, grateful for their very survival.

Stranded on Boon Island

They had spent twenty seven days on the rock known as **Boon Island** before they were rescued. The men were weak and frozen after nearly a month without fresh water, little food, and no fire in the blistering cold. They were walking skeletons. All had frost bite and frozen limbs but they were still alive although many had to have limbs amputated

So there remains, somewhere near Boon Island near Star Island, the scattered wreckage of the *Nottingham,* close nearby, is an iron safe containing a fortune in rare rubies

Nottingham breaking up on the rocks

waiting for some lucky person to find them.

Duck Island Lone Survivor Tells of Money Chest

In March 1876, only one person survived a shipwreck of an unidentified brig that crashed behind White Island. The schooner *Birkmyre* hit Duck Island in March 1875, losing two of its crew and a substantial amount of money in a chest which has not been recovered

Treasure in Casco Bay

Where might it be found?

Almost all of the 126 islands in Casco Bay have been connected
with buried treasures in one way or another, mostly pirate
booty connected with Lowe, Kidd, Dixie Bull, and Blackbeard.

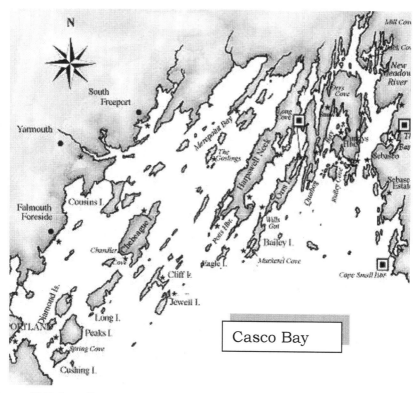

Casco Bay

Jewell Island

Jewell's Island on the outer fringe of Casco Bay, was a favorite
haunt of smugglers and pirates dating back to the 1600's. It has
been a legend from the earliest times that there is pirate
treasure buried somewhere on the small 221-acre island.

Piles of flat stones reaching 4-5 feet high can be found here. It is
believed by some that the stones are markers left by pirates
that, with a proper map, would indicate the direction of a
buried treasure.

It is reported that Captain Kidd, fearing imminent capture, is
said to have put ashore and buried his treasure on Jewell

Island. He then marked the spot with either a square flat rock or reversed compass carved on a tree. He is reported to have made a map for finding his hoard of gold and jewels. The map has not been found.

However,

A chest of treasure was recovered from Jewell Island on the SE shore sometime around 1850. Perhaps part of Captain Kidd's treasure?

In 1901, two seamen from Nova Scotia came to Jewell Island with an ancient map, perhaps that belonging to Captain Kidd. They dug for a supposed cache of pirate treasure, excavated a large hole, and then vanished. Years later, another party of treasure seekers while digging for treasure, unearthed the

skeleton of a man with his skull crushed in from behind as if it were struck by a shovel. The remains were believed to be those of one of the Nova Scotia seamen of the 1850's.

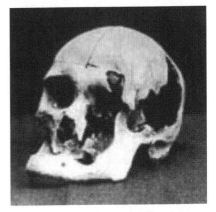

Crushed skull

A second pirate, smuggler and schooner Captain Jonathan Chase, is also a part of Jewell Island pirate lore. Chase, who lived on Jewell Island, is suspected of hiding or burying caches of money in or near his old house.

It is said that Chase would post lanterns to lure innocent ships unfamiliar with Maine's waters onto the rocky shore. Chase and his men would then plunder the wreck scooping up anything of value and murdering any surviving crew.

After his death, a search of his home and grounds revealed empty secret compartments, sliding panels and underground passages in his house, but no treasure was found.

Jewell Island can be reached by private boat or the Portland Express Water Taxi.

Cliff Island

This island was once the home of a tough bachelor and old salvager called Captain Keiff. He lived alone in a log hut on the island. His favorite way to wreck ships was to tie a lantern to his horse's neck, then ride up and down the shoreline. Ships at sea would be misguided by this light and be wrecked on the reefs and ledges that surrounded the island.

Keiff would kill any survivors of the wrecks, and then salvage the cargo. In those days, while it wasn't encouraged, illegal salvaging was condoned, and no questions were asked when someone sold salvaged goods.

Keiff is supposed to have made a fortune in his nefarious occupation. It is known that he buried a large cache of money somewhere on the island that has never been found. Some estimates place the value of this treasure at $400,000. How many millions is that in today's money? There is a place on the island still known as Keiffs Gardens.

Most of Keiff's money is supposedly still buried. This is quite possible, since he had no family and lived alone with very few ways to spend money, as the wrecked ships supplied him with most of his needs.

Pirates burying treasure in a pit

Treasure and relic hunters find Cliff Island, especially after storms, a prime search area because of all the shipwrecks offshore,

The pirate Captain Kidd is said to have buried a cache of treasure in a pit on Cliff Island.

Bailey Island,

In Casco Bay, there is a well-authenticated story of pirate treasure actually having been found in the 1850s. A farmer named John Wilson was duck hunting on the island when, in an attempt to retrieve a fallen bird, he slipped into a crevice between two ledges. In his scramble to climb out, he uncovered a copper kettle filled with pieces of Spanish gold. He exchanged these for $12,000 in coin of the day (about $500,000 today), a comfortable fortune at that time. Dates on the coins indicated the find was not Captain Kidd's treasure. Is Captain Kidd's treasure still there to be found?

Copper kettle with gold coins

Damariscotta Island

Located near Kennebec, Maine, is a lake of salt water, which, like dozens of shallow ones in this country, is locally reputed to be bottomless. Yet Kidd was believed to have sunk some of his valuables there, and to have guarded against the entrance of boats by means of a chain hung from rock to rock at the narrow entrance, bolts on either side showing the points of attachment, while ring bolts were thought to have been driven for the purpose of tying buoys, thus marking the spots where the chests went down. This island, too, is considered by many as "haunted ground."

Cedar Ledges east of **Ram Island** in Casco Bay, three kettles of gold coins were found on Thanksgiving Day, 1852, and more may still be there.

Haskell Island

The island is located near Harpswell Neck and is reported to be one of several places along the Maine coast that Captain Kidd is supposed to have hidden some of his treasure. According to the "Folklore of Maine" in the Library of the Maine Historical Society, the Haskell brothers, one brother took ill and the other rowed to the mainland to get medical help.

While he was gone several of Captain Kidd's former pirates came to the island and found the Captain's treasure but were discovered by the ailing Haskell brother. To keep their secret the bounty hunters killed and slashed the Haskell brother to pieces in an attempt to make it look as though the island's wild bob cats had done the gruesome deed.

Wild cat

Did the bounty hunters find all of Captain Kidd's hidden treasure?

Matinicus –

Often referred to as the *pirate* island because; in the spring of 1717 the pirate ships *Anne* and *Fisher,* being survivors of the fierce storm of April 26, 1717 that sank pirate Samuel Bellamy's treasure laden ship the *Whydah* off of a Cape Cod beach, used the island as a base to attack vessels in the area as they awaited Bellamy's arrival.

While the pirates waited at Matinicus:

> "....... *they took a sloop belonging to Colonel [Stephen] Minot, one shallop belonging to Capt. [John] Lane and three Schooners. They brought the Sloop and Shallop and (as we are informed) the sails and compasses of the 3 schooners to Menhagen [Monhegan], whereupon they manned the last mentioned Sloop with ten hands...*"

The pirates departed the area on May 9, 1717, on the 25-ton sloop formerly belonging to Colonel Minot, with a pirate crew of 19.

Damariscove Island

Dixie Bull, an English sea captain descended from an aristocratic family, was the first pirate known to prey upon shipping off the northeastern colonies, especially along the rocky coast of Maine. Some of his hidden hoards have contributed to the traditions of pirates and buried treasure along the New England coast.

One of his treasures was reputed to be worth $400,000 at the time of its burial on Damariscove Island. If found today, its value could be worth $4,000,000 or more in today's dollars.

Cushing Island

Another of his hoards is supposed to have been buried on Cushing Island. Neither trove is known to have been recovered.

Pinnace under sail

Bull was a native of London who came to Boston in 1631. He was associated with Sir Ferdinando Gorges in development of a large land grant east of Agamonticus at York, Maine. He rapidly adapted to the rugged life of the New Worlds wilderness, becoming a trader in beaver pelts with the Indians.

In June 1631, while trading in the Penobscot Bay area, Bull was attacked by a roving band of Frenchmen in a pinnace, or small sailing ship. They seized his sloop and stock of coats, rugs, blankets, biscuits, etc. This same band captured the Plymouth Company's Castine trading post which was filled with other valuable loot.

Trader Bull, fired by a desire for revenge, assembled 20 men to prey upon French shipping in an effort to recoup his loss. Their attempts were unsuccessful, for the French had temporarily ceased their raids. Bull's food and supplies were running low, so

244

he attacked and plundered three small English vessels in order to keep operating.

These attacks put him in serious trouble with the Crown, and he became desperate. His next escapade was later in 1632, when he sailed into the harbor of Pemaquid, sacked the trading post and nearby dwellings, and escaped with $2,500.

There was little resistance to the attack, but while loading goods aboard his sloop, someone on shore fired a musket and Bull's second in command was struck in the chest, killing him. Until then, many of the crew had considered piracy a lark. Now it suddenly became deadly serious business.

Early in February 1633, three of Bull,s crew secretly returned to their Maine homes. They said Bull had sailed eastward and joined the French, his former enemies. Another statement by a Captain Roger Clap indicated that Bull eventually returned to England. His destiny is lost in the maze of history. One version says that he was finally captured and hung at Tyburn, England.

Bull's fate will probably never be known. The fate of his buried treasure on Cushing and Damariscove Islands may be determined by a skillful treasure hunter.

John's Island

A Portuguese seaman was known to frequent a tavern on the N end of John's Island in Casco Bay. Before he died, he reportedly drew a map showing the location of a hidden well somewhere behind the tavern where he had secreted a cache of $50,000 in gold and silver coins. His treasure has never been recovered.

Great Island

The pirate Captain Linnacum buried a cache of pirate treasure on either Sebascodegan or Great Island in Casco Bay.

Gott's Island

Gott's Island was a hiding place for pirates in the early days. There is supposed to be a substantial cache of gold coins buried somewhere on the island.

Elm Island

In 1840, an old, iron kettle full of $10,000 in coins was found in a hole on Elm Island in Casco Bay.

Haskell Island

A pot containing $1,800 in gold coins was found by a farmer plowing his field in the 1860's on Haskell Island.

Great Chebeague Island

A former member of a pirate band arrived on Great Chebeague Island in search of a cache of treasure buried by his former companions. He was unable to locate the treasure and left the island.

Great Island

The pirate Captain Linnacum is said to have buried several caches of treasure in and around Sebascodegan, or Great Island about 1775.

Orr's Island

The story is that while Captain Kit was plowing his field he struck what reports described as a "pot of gold." He and his eleven children lived the good life thereafter.

Another legend has Pirate treasure buried in the area of Smuggler's Cove, at the N end of Long Cove, on Orr's Island.

Great Chebeague Island

Can be reached by ferry from Falmouth to Portland, is the second-largest island in Casco Bay.

In the 1860s, an old sailor said that in his pirate days he had been one of a pirate crew which many years before had buried a great treasure here. He began digging in a secluded part of the island. One day, a young islander offered to assist him. When the offer was curtly refused, the islander leaped over the rope with which the old man had enclosed the spot where he was digging; whereupon the treasure seeker, in a voice quaking with anger, cried, I call on God and you people to witness that within a year this young fool will be tied in knots, even as I could tie this rope.

No one remembers now whether any treasure was found, but a short time later, the young man was soaked while fishing. He was confined to his bed with an agonizing malady which drew up his arms and legs as if tied in knots, and when he died, soon afterward, it was necessary to break the bones of his limbs in order to get his body into the casket.

Pond Island

Early in the 18th century it is reported that a conscripted sailor escaped from the pirate Captain Lowe's ship "Don Pedro." The ship was carrying a load of jewelry, gold and silver from Mexico to Spain. Somewhere off the coast of New York the pirate's ship was spotted by a British frigate which chased it all the way to Casco Bay where they lost sight of it in a dense fog.

Pond Island Light

The pirates came ashore on Pond Island and are said to have buried their treasure on the island planning to return for it once they were free of the pursuing frigate. The loot, reportedly worth $100,000 in the 1700s, must be worth multi millions today.

Lowe never returned to recover the loot, and was executed by a French court for piracy. A pot of gold coins was found by a farmer on Pond Island so Edward Lowe or other pirates may have regularly hid treasure on this island.

Another Account of Pond Island Treasure

The pirate Edward Lowe is believed to have buried a huge sum of gold coins, silver bars, and jewels in the Harpswell area at both Haskell Island at the South Harpswell Neck and at the edge of a pond on Pond Island in Casco Bay east of Harpswell.

In 1723, he attacked the Spanish ship Don Pedro del Montclova that was traveling from Havana to Spain, commandeered the treasure, and sank the ship. When a British gunboat began pursuing them, Captain Lowe and his men hauled the treasure ashore at the south end of Pond Island in three longboats, and then carried it to the edge of a large pond on the northeast side of the island and tossed the chests, bars of silver, and kegs into the water.

John's Island

One might wonder if there is any truth to the story of treasure on Johns Island, in Casco Bay. Many stories cling to this little island, which is famed as being the summer home of the Lauder family and Gene Tunney. Tradition has it that there was a large frame tavern on the north end of the island, a hangout for seamen.

One of these was a Portuguese who never did any work, but always had plenty of gold and silver to spend when he appeared from

Is treasure hidden at the bottom of the well?

parts unknown. This went on for years. Finally, he died in a foreign land, but before he breathed his last, he gave a friend a map of John's Island, showing the location of a hidden well near the tavern. At the bottom of the well, he said, gold and silver would be found because I helped put it there from the pirate craft *Dare Devil*, commanded by Dixie Bull. Searches have been made for this well, but without success.

Treasure in Penobscot Bay

Deer Isle

Was the New York Astor family's fortune actually founded upon the Pirate Captain William Kidd's treasure found in an iron box (with the initials WK chiseled on the lid) hidden on the property of Mr. Frederick Law Olmsted.

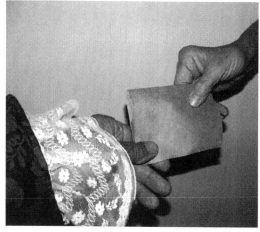

Capt Kidd passes note

Olmstead was a famous landscape architect and designer of New York's *Central Park* and Boston's *"Emerald Necklace."* Is there more treasure to be found on Deer Isle?

Just before Captain Kidd was to be hanged in 1710 and, after a whispered conference with his wife, Kidd was seen handing a small piece of paper to her. The paper bore the mysterious figures "44106818." Could the numbers indicate the longitude 4410 and latitude 6818 and the exact location of the remainder of Captain Kidd's treasure? The latitude for Deer Isle is exactly 4410! Plus, a cave on the Olmsted estate's latitude 6813, very close to the 6818 scribbled on Captain Kidd's final writing before he was hung.

Monroe Island

The island is located off of Owl's Point State Park in Penobscot Bay. For many years this island was reportedly used by pirates and thieves. Treasures are reportedly been hidden all over the island.

Oak Island

Oak Island is located in Penobscot Bay. According to the book "Folklore of Maine," an elderly blind man is reported to have experienced a dream where a barrel of gold rolled out of a cave on a cliff into a pond below. His description matched that of a place on Oak Island where a pond lay below a cliff with a cave. The pond was dragged for a week but the gold filled barrel was not found. There are those who still believe that gold is there waiting to be found.

Great Duck Island

Great Duck is a 237 acre island located at sea approximately 10 miles south of Mt Desert Island. The northeast end of the island consists of cliffs and ledges, but ironically contains the only "all-weather" landing spot.

William Bigenho, who purchased the island in 1951, had identified it as the island on a 16th or 17th century "treasure map."

His daughter later reported that her parents discovered a treasure consisting of gold, silver, and various artifacts. They were lead to the site of the treasure by a combination of the map and various signs carved on rocks, perhaps including a reversed compass.

Pirate treasure unearthed on Maine Island?

Bucksport area

Jean Vincent de Abadie, Baron de St. Castine, was a French nobleman who inherited land on Penobscot Bay in what is now the state of Maine. He took possession in 1665 and ran a successful trading post at the village of Pentagoet for nearly 25 years, amassing a fortune.

In 1840, Captain Stephen Grindle and his son Samuel were hauling logs to the Penobscot River Narrows, (an area near Bucksport) about six miles from the village, when they found a coin, a French crown. The pair dug until dark, recovering 20 more coins. It was in late November, and during the night a severe blizzard struck, so digging was suspended until the spring of 1841.

Returning in the spring, the Grindles dug up nearly 500 coins from France, Spain, South America, Portugal, Holland, England, and Massachusetts. Was this the de Castine hoard, missing for 137 years?

The collection also contained 150 Pine Tree shillings and sixpence dated 1652. This was the first coinage struck in the colonies. The Pine Tree shillings are valued up to $2,000 each.

It was reported in 1855 that a man named Connolly, another Narrows resident, found an old chest with the remains of clothing and other goods.

Records show Baron de St. Castine fled with six money chests. Thus far, only one has reportedly been found. Records further indicate that a year before the Barons flight, a French visitor had estimated the treasure to be worth $200,000. Over three hundred years have passed. What is the value of those five missing chests today?

Sunken Treasure aboard Circus Ship

For those interested in sunken treasure, somewhere in Penobscot Bay, Maine, not far from Vinalhaven, are the charred remains of the 164 foot side-wheeler *Royal Tar*, and her treasure chest of $35,000 in gold and silver.

This is the story of a vessel that caught fire east of Fox Island in Penobscot Bay and later drifted off and sank. The ship carried 85 passengers and a menagerie of circus animals, 32 persons and all of the animals perished. The ship left St. John, New Brunswick and was headed toward Portland, ME in the year 1886.

A circus, returning to the States after a highly successful summer tour of New Brunswick, chartered the *Royal Tar* for the voyage home. The circus was almost too big to fit on the ship. Several of the *Royal Tars* lifeboats were removed in order to fit the troupe aboard.

The ship sailed for Portland, Maine, on October 21, 1836, riding very low in the water, her decks crowded with circus animals, including a gigantic Indian elephant.

As the steamer lay at anchor about two miles off the Fox Island thoroughfare in Penobscot Bay, the ship burst into flames. The fire grew with lightning speed and soon was beyond control and the captain ordered the few lifeboats filled and lowered.

Seven hours after the fire had begun; the *Royal Tar* sank beneath the waves. It is estimated that, in the meantime, she had drifted some 20 miles, as the captain had pulled the anchor.

The $35,000 in the pursers safe was untouched by anyone during the fire. It is understandable that all concerned had to abandon the ship too hastily to think about saving the money. At least, this was the report of all those questioned following the disaster.

So the treasure was still on board the *Royal Tar* when she sank, and the facts seem to indicate that it is still there, on the bottom of Penobscot Bay with an estimated value, in today's dollars, of $3,500,000.

Treasure in Boothbay

Outer Heron Island

Outer Heron Island lies a few miles offshore from Boothbay Harbor.

Around 1900, two young men came to Outer Heron Island from New York. They had a map of the island showing where a chest of pirate gold was supposedly buried. The two never revealed how this map came into their possession. With a specially constructed auger that could be lengthened indefinitely by adding

Pirate's Map?

sections of iron rod, they started boring near a lone, grotesquely-shaped spruce tree on the highest point of the island.

After a month of constant work, and at a depth of 30 feet, the auger brought up oaken chips. They penetrated this, and the bit came up with particles of what seemed to be gold. The two then hired two Italian laborers and excavated a 30-foot shaft. At this depth, a 6-foot oak plank was found, and that was all. The gold had come from a copper spike which the auger point had rapped.

The mystery is how did a copper spike and a six-foot plank get 30 feet underground, unless some kind of excavating had been done years before? No report of any treasures being found in the area can be located.

Swan's Island

Swan's Island is located in the Kennebec River and is reported to be the site of another pirate cache.

Blackbeard boarding ship

Treasure -Mid Coast Maine

Manana Island

Found off the middle coast of Maine. Around 1900, several fishermen stopped their boat at this island to relax. They decided to play a game of soccer. When a wild kick was made by one of the crew-members, the captain of the group ran to retrieve the ball.

As he picked up the ball, he noticed rusty metal sticking out of the sand. He dug the sand from around the object, and saw that it was an old iron pot filled with coins. Since he was out of sight of his crew, he stuck the pot into a nearby rock crevice, intending to come back for it later.

After playing for a while longer, the crew went back to their fishing boat. The captain made an excuse to stay behind for a short time. Returning to what he thought was the crevice where he had put the pot of coins; he was amazed that he could not find the right one. Deciding that part of the coins would be better than none, the captain called his crew and told them what he had done.

The entire company spent several hours in search of the coins, but were never able to find them. As far as is known, somewhere on Manana Island, stuck in a rock crevice, there is a cache of coins waiting for a lucky treasure hunter.

255

Pirates demand booty after sacking the town
By Howard Pyle - 1900

Macias Region
A Favorite with Pirates

Pirate Captain Rhodes

If you are ever in the areas of the coastal town of Machias, you will hear tales of loot hidden by the notorious pirate, Captain Rhodes. He roamed this shore in 1675, using the sheltered inlet of the Machias River as a hideout and a place for careening his ship.

Pirate Captains Harry Thompson and Starbird

Another Machias area treasure is stashed along Starbirds Creek. Years ago, Captain Harry Thompson and another buccaneer named Starbird frequently used the entrance to the Machias River as a rendezvous between voyages. As a consequence, they used a nearby creek, named for Starbird, to cache their plunder.

Thompson was said to have marked some trees and to have drawn a crude map to aid his children in locating this trove, but they apparently misinterpreted the clues, for they dug without success.

The Brothers Flynn

In the same general area, Brothers Island, named for two brothers called Flynn, is reputedly a hiding place for their treasure trove. However, information concerning this cache is not easy to establish.

Monhegan Island,

Being located miles out to sea off the mainland, Monhegan Island is a natural for pirates. Captain Bellamy, "the richest pirate," is said to have hidden some of his treasure "somewhere on the island."

Samuel Bellamy and Paulsgrave Williams

There reportedly is a hidden underground vault containing pirate treasure in the vicinity of the Machias River. Legend says that the Pirate, Black Bellamy built the vault beneath his wooden fort on the river. The fort is now gone, but it was known to be located near the bridge on State route A1.

Bellamy's Jolly Roger

Other version reports the treasure mouth of the Machias River is not where the two pirates had their stronghold, but further upriver. They did dig a subterranean treasure house, but it was not inside the fort. There is little doubt but that the vault holds a large hoard of treasure to this day.

After looting a number of ships, the pirates arrived at a destination selected by Captain Bellamy, the only navigator on board. The spot was near the mouth of the Machias River, far from any civilized community at that time. It was here that Bellamy and Williams put their plan into action. The cargo had to be hidden very well before they sailed to continue their pirating.

A large vault was excavated to serve as a treasure house and their treasure secreted. When all of this was done, and the *Whydah* had been overhauled, Bellamy and Williams set sail again. After several forays, the treasure house was filled.

The headquarters of Bellamy and Williams, near the mouth of the Machias River, has disappeared. But somewhere nearby is hidden one of the richest pirate caches in North America, one that has never been reported found.

Black Sam Bellamy, the Robin hood of the Sea, had the stereotype Jolly Roger.

Finding Relics and Old Coins

A few tips from the pros

Recovering older more valuable coins plus holding in your hands different relics of the past will be something you will want to experience. Finding coins from the 17th, 18th and early 19th Century is a far greater thrill then you can imagine.

The answer to finding older sites is "Research!" Where can you find research material?

1-Old Maps - can be found in local libraries, local history books, they show old roads, abandoned railroad stations, many times school buildings and other points of interest that either no longer exist, or people have forgotten about.

2-Old Newspapers contain a wealth of information on almost every page Stories about holiday celebration on the town square park (May no longer exists) Carnival arriving in town (where did they set up?) and much more information.

3-Old Property Tax Records show where older houses, farms, service stations, interstate bus stops, taverns etc.. once stood.

4-Local Historical Societies are a great resource containing valuable information on dozens of older happenings of your town from its very beginnings up till today.

5-Local Museums usually have displays of historical interest as well as many books on the area's history. Spend time with anyone that works in the museum, they generally are part "Historian."

6- Librarians can direct you to a wealth of information about your town. Libraries are the main "Depository" of information of all kinds,, many times having a number of items discussed above, "old maps, old books, old records, etc".

A Pirates life for me
By Howard Pyle

Pirates Used "Magic Rods" to Locate Treasure and More

Locate Sunken or Buried Treasure, Water Veins, Underground Pipes, Lost Children and Pets, Murderers, Thieves, Liars and Much More

In 1588 the defeat of the Spanish Armada brought the Spanish Galley *Florencia* into the harbor of Tobermory Bay in northern Scotland. She was badly damaged during battle and shortly after dropping her anchor in the harbor the ship exploded and sank. It was widely reported to have been heavily laden with gold and silver which today would be valued at Thirty Three Million Dollars.

A Spanish Galleon of the era

Captain William Kidd, before becoming a famous pirate, was a successful businessman in Glashow, Scotland. Kidd employed a "dowser" from Yorkshire, England to search for the treasure ship *Florencia* of Tobermory Bay.

The dowser was reportedly not only able to locate sunken or buried treasure but could also tell what was being detected by the rods: gold, silver, or copper.

M. de Vallemont, wrote in 1706:

"But, with the divining rod, it is possible to distinguish what metal is contained in the mine towards which the rod inclines. For if a gold coin be placed in each hand, the rod will only turn in the direction of gold, because it becomes impregnated with the corpuscles or minute particles of gold. If silver be treated in the same way, the rod will only dip towards silver. This, at any rate, is what we are told by those who pride themselves on their successful use of the rod."

261

Dowsing using rods, forked branches and other devices dates back to ancient times and the era BC.

The very scholarly Abbé Le Lorrain de Vallemont of France who in 1693 published *La Physique Occulte,* or "Treatise on the Divining Rod and its Uses for the Discovery of Springs of Water, Metallic Veins, Hidden Treasure, Thieves, and Escaped Murderers" is quoted as saying:

"If one desires to find pirates' gold, it is really essential to believe in the divining rod and devoutly obey its magic messages."

Combine an Ancient Method with Modern Technology and Locate Lost Treasures

Amongst the many things rods can provide is Yes or No answers to questions asked. Example: "Are there valuables buried in the sand on this beach?" The Rods will answer by swinging to either the Yes or No position.

The Rods will also point to objects you want to find. Using just one Rod say; "Point to the valuables on the beach." The single rod will swing to indicate the direction in which you should travel.

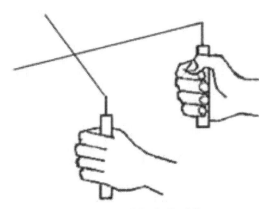

Modern day "Magic Rods" in the No position

You can then either continue using the rods to uncover the treasure or switch to a modern day metal detector to complete the task of discovery. Should you decide to continue by using the Rods simply hold the two rods parallel to the ground and walk slowly in the direction the rods have indicated. The Rods will swing open when you are over the buried items.

Locate Lost Animals, Children and More

To find the lost animal or child etc simply ask "Where is Fluffy?" and the single Rod will swing to the direction you should travel. We were at our cabin in northern Maine one January with our new puppy. In the hustle and bustle of unloading the skiing gear, food, luggage etc, Skipper wandered off somewhere.

We were the only people at the lake on the edge of the White Mountain National Forest that January. Which way did Skipper wander? With no one to ask if they had seen him; which way should we go to find the little pooch? You guessed it; our "Magic Rods" came to the rescue. Skipper had crossed over the frozen lake and we found him right where the Rods indicated; huddled under the porch of a vacant cottage.

Thieves, Murderers, Rapists and Liars

Odds are you will not have a need to use your Rods to identify the type of nefarious individuals above however; you may have a more mundane yet handy application for them. For example; while on your family treasure hunt at the beach you discover someone ate your lunch! All you need to do is assemble your group and ask the Rods "Who ate my sandwich?" and the Rods will do the rest.

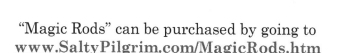

"Magic Rods" can be purchased by going to
www.SaltyPilgrim.com/MagicRods.htm

263

Finding Treasure on Beaches

Vacationers bring "Treasure" to beaches daily

Valuables found on the beach may have been dropped by a vacationer or washed ashore from a sunken ship. Beach hunting is probably the only form of treasure hunting where almost anyone can go and find items worth $100's or even $1,000's.

The following tips will help you become successful in beach and water treasure detecting:.

- **The areas where mothers splash around with their toddlers** - Suntan lotion, cool water and splashing often combine to loosen rings that find their way off fingers.

- **The areas where teens and adults tend to horse around:** suntan lotion and horseplay tends to result in items being lost.

- **The dry sand:** Where chairs and towels are laid out, volleyball nets, around concession stands

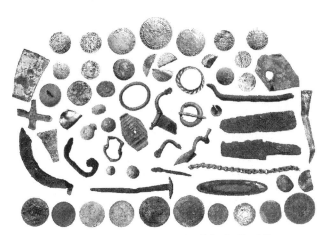

Found on the Beach with "Magic Rods"

Resources

Charles Johnson (1724). *A General History of the Pyrates.*

Treasure Island by Robert Louis Stevenson—

Captain Blood by Rafael Sabatini,

Emilio Salgari , *The Black Corsair*)

Jade Parker, "To Catch A Pirate"

Dan Conlin.. *Pirates of the Atlantic: Robbery, murder and mayhem off the Canadian East Coast* Halifax

Ellms, Charles. The Project Gutenberg eBook, *The Pirates Own Book*

Botting, Douglas. *The Pirates.* Time-Life,. .

Cordingly, David *Under the Black Flag.*

Defoe, Daniel. *The General History of the Pyrates.*

Earle, Peter. *The Pirate Wars.* St. Martin's

Marley, David F. *Pirates and Privateers of the Americas.*

Pirates: Terror on the High Seas from the Caribbean to the South China Sea.

Rogozinski, Jan. *Honor Among Thieves.*

cindyvallar.com/

A Book of Pirates by Howard Pyle (1858 – 1911)

NationalGeographic.com

thePiratesRealm.com

ageofpirates.com

piratesoul.com

tinpan.fortunecity.com

wikapedia.com

thefreedictionary.com

A Pirate was fearsome fellow
By Howard Pyle - 1898

Other Books by Ted Burbank

- ➤ Cape Cod Shipwrecks - "Graveyard of the Atlantic"
- ➤ Pirates and Treasure on Cape Cod
- ➤ Shipwrecks, Pirates and Treasure in Maine
- ➤ A Homeowner's Complete Guide to Energy Independence
- ➤ The "Islands" of Ocean Bluff and Brant Rock
- ➤ 365 Ways to Unplug Your Kids or *How to have fun without TV or Computers*
- ➤ A Guide to Plymouth's Famous Burial Hill

Any of these books can be ordered from Salty Pilgrim Press by going to www.SaltyPilgrim.com

Need an entertaining and interesting speaker?

Ted is available to provide your club or organization a presentation based upon any of the subjects covered by his books or to participant in your Pirate Festival or Fair.

Ted Burbank

Call: 508.794.1200 to schedule

Considering buying or selling a business?

Go to www.BuySellBiz.com for valuable information and tips gained through the purchase and sale of more than 2,000 private businesses

Made in the USA
Charleston, SC
10 May 2016